Reflections on the target language

Other titles in the series

Language teaching in the mirror
edited by Anthony Peck and David Westgate
REFLECTIONS ON PRACTICE 1

The first title in the series focuses on the why and how of reflecting on classroom practice. Different modes of reflection demonstrated include: evaluations; diary keeping; video action-replay; peer observation; micro-teaching. Subjects chosen for reflection include: language interaction in the classroom; the proportion of target language used in the classroom; implicit and explicit grammar teaching. The final chapter provides guidelines on how to develop a theoretical framework for action research and the practical steps to setting up a project.

Reflections on reading: from GCSE to 'A' level
edited by Mike Grenfell
REFLECTIONS ON PRACTICE 2

Three practising teachers consider approaches to reading in a foreign language at intermediate and advanced level in schools and colleges. The first charts the reading habits of a Year 9 class as they move from beginner to intermediate levels. The other two are concerned with the problems learners face in bridging the gap between GCSE and 'A' level, especially when encountering literary texts, and explore strategies which can help to overcome the difficulties.

Reflections on modern languages in primary education: six case studies
edited by Alison Hurrell and Peter Satchwell
REFLECTIONS ON PRACTICE 3

Six teachers present their reflections on foreign language teaching and learning at primary level in the UK. Areas covered include progression from primary to secondary, integrating the foreign language into the primary curriculum and teaching in two languages.

CILT Publications are available from Grantham Book Services, Isaac Newton Way, Alma Park Industrial Estate, Grantham, Lincs, NG31 9SD.

Telephone: 01476 541 080, Fax: 01476 541 061.

Reflections on practice

Series editor: Richard Johnstone

Reflections on the target language

Peter S Neil

Centre for Information
on Language Teaching and Research

The views expressed in this book are those of the author and do not necessarily reflect the views of CILT.

First published 1997
Copyright © 1997 Centre for Information on Language Teaching and Research
ISBN 1 874016 80 1

A catalogue record for this book is available from the British Library
Printed in Great Britain by Bourne Press Ltd
Cover by Neil Alexander

Published by the Centre for Information on Language Teaching and Research,
20 Bedfordbury, Covent Garden, London WC2N 4LB

CILT Publications are available from: Grantham Book Services, Isaac Newton Way, Alma Park Industrial Estate, Grantham, Lincs NG31 8SD. Tel: 01476 541 000. Fax: 01476 541 060. Book trade representation (UK and Ireland): Broadcast Book Services, 24 De Montfort Road, London SW16 1LZ. Tel: 0181 677 5129.

Published by the Centre for Information on Language Teaching and Research, 20 Bedfordbury, Covent Garden, London WC2N 4LB.

Contents

Acknowledgements

I should like to thank a number of individuals without whose help this book would not have been possible: the principals, heads of modern languages, teachers and pupils in the ten schools for allowing me to visit the departments, interview, survey and record the material; Mr T D Johnstone, Principal Inspector of Modern Languages at the Department of Education for Northern Ireland; the native-speakers of German, in particular Doris Gentemann who spent weeks transcribing tapes and offering advice on the authenticity of the language; my exchange students from Paderborn, Germany (Heidi Kienz, Bianka Hortig and Tanja Beerens) for their helpful comments; Dr Ros Mitchell and Prof Barbara Wing for their encouragement in carrying out the project and for granting permission to use parts of their studies. Finally I should like to acknowledge the support of my colleagues John Salters and Dr Alex McEwen throughout the project, and of Mrs J Neill for proofreading the manuscript.

List of tables

Preface

Dr Peter Neil's *Reflections on the target language* is the fourth in CILT's REFLECTIONS ON PRACTICE series. It is concerned with the use of the foreign language in secondary school classrooms, something that for several years now has been strongly recommended by national curricular guidelines within the UK but that continues to confront busy classroom teachers with real problems.

In at least two ways, the present study is different from previous studies in the series. First, the context of the study is limited to one part of the UK, namely Northern Ireland, and there is only one foreign language involved, namely German. Second, the text has been written by one writer who specialises in teacher education and research. It has not been written by multiple authors, including schoolteachers themselves.

Nonetheless, the text is entirely faithful to the key principles of the series:

- it has been skilfully written in such a way as to be accessible to a readership anywhere in the UK or beyond that has an interest in the teaching and learning of languages in institutional contexts, including (I would say) further and higher education as well as schools, rather than limited to those from one part of the UK, favouring one particular language and working in one particular type of institution;

- it could not have been written without substantial and continuing collaboration with classroom teachers. Far from being the mere objects of a researcher's research, they were clearly an essential ingredient in the research process.

A further characteristic of Peter Neil's text is that it builds on the substantial body of international, published research dealing with foreign language use in classrooms. As such it enables us to see his own study within a much wider research context. We gain a sense of what is new and different and of what is common to previous studies. At the same time it enables us to reflect on practical classroom applications in contexts that may be very different from the particular one that is described.

I am sure that this carefully researched, academically sound yet highly practical text will be of benefit to teachers, researchers, advisers and teacher educators who are keen to reflect on the possible use of the foreign language in languages classrooms and on its possible relations with learners' first language.

Professor Richard Johnstone
Series Editor: REFLECTIONS ON PRACTICE

Introduction

Since the implementation of the National Curriculum in England and Wales, the 5–14 Guidelines in Scotland and the Common Curriculum in Northern Ireland, a greater emphasis has been placed on the use of the target language by teachers and by pupils in the foreign language classroom. Many official curriculum documents refer to it:

> *The first essential is frequent contact with the target language through the teacher's continuous use of it and through tape recordings [. . .]* (DES/WO, 1990, par 9.5)

> *In pursuing [the aims of modern language learning] most teaching programmes incorporate the following features: the development of communicative competence among the pupils, the increasing use of the foreign language as the medium of the classroom [. . .]* (SOED, 1991: 2)

> *The target language can be used both to practise specific language patterns and vocabulary and to communicate with the pupils on everyday topics in modern language classes.* (NICC, 1992, par. 8.3)

Even before the current developments, however, department inspectors in Northern Ireland recommended extended use of the target language as an indicator of good practice:

> *The lesson should be conducted through the medium of the target language, to provide adequate aural and oral practice and also to avoid interference from the sound and syntactical patterns of the mother tongue. It will also help to lessen any desire the pupils may have to engage in the process of translation rather than to respond instinctively in the target language to an aural or visual stimulus.* (DENI, 1985, par 3.1)

Despite the fact it is not stated outright in these documents that teachers should make exclusive use of the foreign language, many teachers assume that they must speak in the target language 100% of the time and that any use of English is indicative of a poor lesson. This perception is perhaps caused by inspectors' reports which comment favourably on lessons in which exclusive use is made of the foreign language:

> *An example of good use of the target language, was seen in a year 9 German class [. . .] conducted entirely in German.* (DENI 1994, par. 4.13.6)

Although this statement, and others like it, simply report that a lesson which was effective just happened to be taught entirely through the target language (it might have been equally effective had there been some instances where English was used), many teachers regard it as a ban on the mother tongue from the classroom. Other practising teachers, however, have come to realise that this is a misunderstanding (Bleasdale, 1995) and that the effective teaching of foreign languages may involve certain phases during lessons where it is appropriate to use English. A recent survey of teachers in the UK reveals that few consider exclusive use of the target language appropriate at Key Stages 3 or 4 (Dickson, 1996). The phrase which is written into many departmental schemes of work is *'judicious use should be made of the target language'*. It appears necessary, therefore, to investigate just what is understood by the ubiquitous term 'judicious' and to discover the extent to which teachers actually use the target language in their normal classroom discourse.

The place of the target language is, however, well established within Communicative Language Teaching, details of which can be found in several works (Littlewood, 1981; Das (ed), 1985; Swan, 1985a, 1985b; Johnstone, 1987; Nunan, 1989). Quantity of target language cannot be equated with quality, however. The excerpt from the inspector's report quoted earlier could refer to both, although there appears to be more weight given to the quantity. Recent conversations with school inspectors and with staff who have just undergone inspections reveal that there appears now to be a change in emphasis from the early days of communicative language teaching when the attention was put on increasing the amount of target language used by teachers, towards a focus on the quality or type of language used.

In the early stages of teaching the language to younger classes, teachers have been seen to make considerable use of simple language, especially for greetings and for issuing classroom instructions (for example see Mitchell, 1986, 1988; Franklin, 1990). (Previous studies on the target language are reviewed in Appendix G.) With older pupils we might expect that the quantity of target language should be maintained but with the complexity increased; anecdotal evidence would suggest, however, that this is not taking place (Mitchell, personal communication) a suspicion which has been confirmed by recent summary reports from OFSTED:

> *The target language is used more by teachers in Key Stage 3 than in Key Stage 4, but its use by pupils is underdeveloped in both Key Stages.* (OFSTED, 1995: 3)

Research which has been carried out in other UK classrooms on teachers' use of the foreign language has been based in the lower school, however, and these studies have focused exclusively on the use of French. This study examines the use of the target language by teachers of German with older pupils, namely those in fourth and fifth form (i.e. those in Key Stage 4). In addition to analysing the target language from the teachers' and researcher's standpoint, it also includes pupils' perceptions, since they are, after all, the consumers of the target language used in the classroom.

The present study sets out to examine the following questions, therefore:

- What are teachers' views on using the target language?
- How do pupils at Key Stage 4 perceive their teachers' use of the language?
- For which parts of the lesson do teachers use the target language and for which English?
- Which strategies do teachers use to make the language accessible to pupils?

BACKGROUND TO THE STUDY

Within the Northern Ireland curriculum pupils are obliged to study one foreign language. German is very much the third or fourth foreign language after French, Irish and Spanish. The pupils in this study, therefore, would generally be more able.

TEACHERS INVOLVED

Since the use of the target language is such a sensitive issue in schools, the researcher had to work with teachers who were willing to participate in the study. Consequently, the sample of teachers involved in the project was not random; ten teachers of German with pupils in Key Stage 4 in grammar schools in Northern Ireland were invited to participate. Details of schools and teachers can be found in Appendix A (they are referred to as T1 to T10 in the study). German was the main foreign language of most of the teachers (the remainder having equal qualifications in French), which meant that they were all interested in the topic under investigation. They would not describe themselves as 'super-teachers' who were doing anything spectacular in terms of the target language in their lessons; in fact, many apologised at the outset. The words of one teacher echo the sentiments of many:

> *I don't know if I'm the right person for this [video-recording]. I'll just be teaching as normal and I won't be making any allowances for the camera. I hope it will be of some help, but I'll be doing my own thing.*

In order to get as complete a picture as possible of the German spoken by the teachers in the lessons, a three-pronged approach was adopted. Ten lessons were recorded on video for subsequent analysis. At the end of the recording period, interviews were conducted with the teachers in which they were asked about their views on the use of the target language. This was followed by their completing a self-report form in which they indicated their perception of their own use of German and English for certain areas of work within lessons. In addition to obtaining information from the teachers and from the observed data, the pupils in the classes under investigation were asked for their perceptions, both by interview and by questionnaire.

The project sought, therefore, to gain a three-dimensional view of the target language being used in the classroom. It was important that the teachers felt very much part of the project and the findings were shown to them at several points in the study. This enabled them to look at their own performance and to compare that with the performance of their colleagues (anonymously). The project teachers were asked for their reaction to the findings and how they felt about their own German classes.

The results of the study are presented in the following chapters. In Chapter 1 the teachers' own views of the target language, as expressed in the interviews and questionnaires, are presented. Chapter 2 then analyses the pupils' views of their teachers' use of the target language, and Chapter 3 opens the door on the observed lessons and examples of some of the strategies used by teachers are illustrated. Since the strategies used in German could be applied equally to other languages, a translation of the main examples quoted is provided.

Chapter 1

Teacher perspectives

This chapter presents the project teachers' views on use of the target language in general and on their own practice in particular. The first part of the chapter analyses their responses during the interview sessions and the second part gives details of responses to a self-report sheet.

Teachers' interviews

Using interviews can have both advantages and disadvantages. One main advantage is the flexibility they allow to develop issues which arise in the course of discussion. The main disadvantages, on the other hand, are firstly, the possibility of bias on the part of the interviewer and secondly, the possibility that the interviewee might say what he or she thinks the interviewer wants to hear. This was a particular danger in this study, since the teachers had been made aware before the start of the project of the main focus of the investigation. It was stated at the outset of each interview, therefore, that the researcher had no fixed views on the topic and that he was interested in hearing teachers' individual opinions on the use of the target language in general and on their own use of German in normal practice.

The interviews were held towards the end of the video-recordings. Each interview lasted approximately half an hour and was recorded for later analysis. The main topic areas covered, called 'domains', were as follows:

1 the representativeness of the video-recordings;
2 whether the department has a policy on the use of the target language;
3 how the target language is used with pupils of different age groups;
4 the effect use of the target language has on the rapport between teacher and pupils;
5 any content areas which are consistently carried out in English;
6 the feasibility/desirability of input only and a silent period;
7 the role of error correction;
8 the role of grammar;
9 how teachers encourage pupil use of the target language;

10 in-service training needs with regard to the target language;
11 the main factors which influence their practice.

DOMAIN 1 REPRESENTATIVENESS OF VIDEO-RECORDINGS

It was felt necessary to give teachers the opportunity to comment on the video recorded lessons, in order to try and ascertain the extent to which these represented normal practice. Five teachers said the videos represented their normal practice, one teacher added that the pupils would not have responded had they been confronted by a new teaching style **and** a video camera. Another teacher commented that the presence of the camera forced her to be more organised. Two teachers mentioned the fact that they altered their practice for the camera in that they abandoned the usual times set aside during the week when they would use English exclusively in order to consolidate and clarify points of grammar which had arisen in previous lessons. This admission revealed that teachers considered an English-based lesson to be unacceptable for the purposes of this project. All remaining teachers commented that the videos were fairly representative. Two of the teachers with fifth form classes stated that they felt it necessary to use more English for examination practice as the GCSE exams approached. Only one teacher (T7) admitted that the video-recorded lessons represented a stage slightly more advanced than normal practice and commented that the video-lessons portrayed his ideal use of the target language, a stage which he had not quite reached yet.

DOMAIN 2 POLICY OF TARGET LANGUAGE USE

All the teachers claimed that their department had a policy on the use of the target language, which stated, in eight out of the ten cases, that the target language should be used as much as possible, whilst the other two teachers pointed out that it should be used where appropriate. Some heads of department commented that they had assistance provided by in-service courses in formulating a policy. Four teachers raised the issue of the autonomy of the class teacher and stated that the policy would only be effective if teachers put it into practice. One teacher claimed that some staff felt very threatened by the whole topic of the target language and he suggested that it would be better integrated into other areas of work, rather than isolated as a major hurdle which could prove divisive and obstructive.

DOMAIN 3 USE OF THE TARGET LANGUAGE WITH DIFFERENT AGE GROUPS

One of the problems in this question was that pupils begin learning German in different years, so that third form for some schools is the first year of German, whereas in one school (T1), German was now offered in first form.

Some teachers said it was easier to use the target language more with younger pupils than with older ones. Others stated that it was more difficult with the younger ones because of the pupils' lack of linguistic resources. The practicalities of using German with fourth and fifth classes were raised by some; one of the main points was the pupils' previous German learning experience. If they had previously had a teacher who did not use much target language in the class, it was much more difficult for the teacher taking over to implement a policy of optimum target language use. This was evident in the pupils of one teacher (T10) some of whom had been taught by another teacher in previous years. It proved difficult during the early stages of the fourth form to acclimatise them to T10's use of the foreign language. The problem of the examination syllabuses was mentioned in relation to fifth form classes, although one fifth form teacher (T1) stated that she used 90+% German in both fourth and fifth form classes. With sixth form classes some enjoyed the opportunity to converse with the pupils at that level, whereas others commented that parts of the examination syllabuses at 'A' level were rather stifling. One teacher commented that the target language was not used according to the age of the pupils, but was dictated by the type of activity. From the responses to this question it appeared that teachers were aware of their patterns of target language use and had given thought to the reasons for their practice.

DOMAIN 4   THE EFFECT OF TARGET LANGUAGE USE ON THE RAPPORT BETWEEN TEACHER AND PUPIL

Teachers were asked to comment, from their experience, on the assertion that exclusive or considerable use of the target language can affect the relationship between teacher and pupil. Nine out of the ten teachers agreed that too much emphasis on the target language can impede the development of good rapport between teacher and pupil. Some pointed to the artificiality of commencing lessons, particularly with fourth and fifth form classes, with a greeting in the foreign language.

> *I think it is silly starting a class with* 'Guten Morgen alle' *when they have been coming in and talking to me in English about football and other things. It's an artificial start.* (T8)

One teacher stated that the first form had been frightened by too much exposure to German in the early days, particularly as they were in a new school and in an unfamiliar environment. Several teachers commented that rapport can be affected when the pupils get confused or lost because of over-use of the target language, which can lead them to become antagonistic. One teacher stated that pupils became very wary when he tried to increase the amount of target language, so that it had to be increased gradually. **Balance and sensitivity are required.**

Only one teacher commented favourably on the influence of target language use on rapport. T2 stated that it had positive effects, in that the pupils enjoyed shouting to her in the corridor *'Wie geht's?'* which enhanced the relationship between them. Another teacher stated that topics such as talking to pupils about their weekend and holidays, can enhance the rapport, but with younger pupils using the target language to do so can be artificial. With older pupils, however, there comes a stage where the language is no longer a barrier and the discussion can be in either in English or German. Therefore it was a matter of perseverance in the hope that the target language could become the natural means of communication in the language classroom:

> *With my sixth form class sometimes we do not know whether*
> *we are speaking in English or German.* (T10)

DOMAIN 5   CONTENT AREAS CONSISTENTLY CARRIED OUT IN ENGLISH

Only T1 did not mention grammar as the main aspect of the work carried out through English; the reason for this may have been that in her department grammar is taught in an extra lunchtime class outwith the normal timetabled classes. Of the nine teachers who stated that grammar was taught through English, five added that they had a distinct pattern for teaching: they started by demonstrating various examples of the structure which were then practised with the pupils as a whole class; this was followed by a paired activity, an explanation given in German and in English, and finally a note was dictated or written down on the board in English and copied down by the pupils. Two teachers stated that the use of English depended on the class, the attitude of the pupils and the time of day. The teaching of background was mentioned by two although they added that it would depend on the complexity of the topic.

Three teachers claimed that examination skills and those parts of the examination which are answered in English are best taught in that language. One added that in earlier years these skills are tested in German, but that English is necessary more in fifth form as the GCSE time approaches. Surprisingly, one teacher of a fifth form class said that English was needed to practise oral work, which referred to giving clear instructions to pupils in order to enable them to work in pairs/groups.

DOMAIN 6   THE FEASIBILITY/DESIRABILITY OF INPUT ONLY AND
A SILENT PERIOD

Teachers were presented with the hypothetical situation in which they would provide only undiluted German without error correction or grammatical explanations and with pupils given no opportunity for speaking or paired activities, as suggested by the theories of Krashen (1985). All of them regarded input only as either an insufficient way to learn a language or a rather tedious experience both for teachers and pupils. Several teachers indicated that, in order to retain motivation and interest, pupils would have to have something to do, they would need to participate in the lessons and to practise the new vocabulary and/or structures. Two teachers mentioned experience as having shown that an input-only approach cannot possibly work; one commented that pupils have to learn by doing and others stated that speaking in the target language by pupils imprints the foreign language sounds in pupils' minds and is necessary for correct pronunciation of those sounds. The time element was either stated explicitly or implied in statements by T6 and T9. One teacher had experience of the German of the *Gastarbeiter* in Germany and she commented that they were able to understand, but that they were unable to communicate at a level beyond the very basic and they spoke very inaccurately. T9 said that pupils would have to listen *'for years on end'* before they could speak. The audio-lingual approach was given as an example of comprehensible input by one teacher who said that the way she had learned languages did involve lots of input but provided no opportunities for interaction. The requirements of the GCSE examination were mentioned by two as reasons for having to practise speaking in class.

In general, none of the teachers was in favour of a purely input-oriented lesson; all were convinced of the value for the pupils of speaking and the motivation from interacting with each other. They rejected the notion that pupils should sit and listen and learn by imbibing the target language, given the many constraints in the language classroom.

DOMAIN 7   ERROR CORRECTION

The views of all the teachers on this question were contained in the answer given by one teacher. She stated that with GCSE the emphasis is on conveying the message, which makes error correction not as necessary as it had been previously. If pupils are going to learn anything, however, they should learn the correct forms. This teacher drew a distinction between major errors which impede communication and those which are less crucial for communication; whereas errors of the former kind would be corrected, the latter would normally be ignored. If a good pupil were to make a relatively minor error from the communication point of view, it might be helpful to correct him or her. Weaker pupils, on the other hand, would not be corrected as frequently, since this would be demotivating and they would not be able to utter two words without teacher interruption. The value of pairwork and group work in this connection was questioned by one, who was concerned that pupils might reinforce each others' errors, when it is not possible for the teacher to monitor the output. Errors could become imprinted and difficult to eradicate. T10 made a distinction between speaking and writing. Whereas she would be prepared to ignore errors in speaking, written errors would be corrected. The teachers did not see any contradiction between the communicative approach to teaching and error correction, in fact they thought that communication could only be enhanced by correcting and eradicating inaccuracies.

DOMAIN 8   THE ROLE OF GRAMMAR

As with the two previous areas, all teachers once again held more or less similar opinions, namely that grammar is important, although, with the present examination at GCSE it requires less attention. It was felt that the better pupils had to know the rules in order to avoid confusion, and in order to equip them with the necessary structures to be creative with the language and to become independent in using it. Many criticised the GCSE for the fact that it was possible to obtain a good grade without having any formal knowledge of the structure of the language, since marks were awarded for communication only. The result of this was that some pupils wanted to continue studying German to 'A' level because of their good grade achieved at GCSE despite the fact that they would not, in the teacher's opinion, be able to cope. Some teachers did not explain grammar until pupils actually asked for the rules, but most felt it necessary to supplement the grammatical explanations in the course book with extra notes.

DOMAIN 9   ENCOURAGING SPONTANEOUS TARGET LANGUAGE USE
BY PUPILS

A major issue at present is how to encourage pupils to use the target language as the main medium of communication in the classroom, which is, after all, an artificial setting. Teachers were asked how they brought pupils to the point of feeling confident in communicating naturally in the target language. Many teachers provided lists of classroom phrases which were useful for basic functions, such as 'I've forgotten my book'; however, the teacher had to be consistent in insisting on use of the target language. One teacher refused to let her fifth form boys out to play rugby unless they asked permission in German.

Various ideas for displaying phrases in the target language around the class were given, such as lists according to function, for example 'Can I . . ?' with examples; bubbles of short phrases; tapes to take home, were mentioned. One teacher pointed to the benefits of an autonomous learning approach where the pupils are permitted to take tapes and record on the PALE system. (Peripheral Audio Learning Equipment is a set of self-standing cassette boxes around a classroom, which enable pupils to work independently of the teacher, either speaking or listening, working individually, in pairs or in groups.)

Another teacher spoke in more general terms about encouraging spontaneous utterances from the pupils:

> It is something to aim to get to, by tipping the balance. Below a certain level of target language use the exercise remains artificial, but once you get beyond a certain level it is possible.
> (T7)

Spontaneity in pupil target language use was mentioned by all teachers as something which they had not yet achieved to a satisfactory level, certainly not in the fourth and fifth years, where motivation was affected by self-consciousness and adolescent reticence.

DOMAIN 10 IN-SERVICE TRAINING

The most useful form of in-service training for improving use of the target language mentioned by all teachers would be a sabbatical term spent in the target country, to brush up not only on the language but also on the cultural aspects. At present such courses are offered to teachers requiring retraining; it was felt, however, that such courses would also benefit those who were competent in the language. Teachers were generally satisfied with the support received from the in-service training provided. Some of the INSET providers had produced booklets on using the target language and courses had been held by various groups.

The point that the target language should not be isolated as a priority *per se*, but should be integrated into other areas requiring in-service training, was reiterated by T7. This way it does not become a stumbling-block to teachers, blown out of proportion to the rest of the work.

DOMAIN 11 INFLUENCES ON PRACTICE

The final question in the interview was intended to gain a global picture of how teachers' practice is influenced. Various factors were mentioned: the influence of head of department, colleagues, the course book, post-graduate training, student teachers, experience, examination syllabuses, the motivation to convey to pupils the love of the language, the methodology of English teaching in Germany and Austria which appeared to be so successful. Involvement with this research project had influenced one teacher's use of the target language, since it caused her to think more about what she was doing!

SUMMARY OF INTERVIEWS

Although not all teachers expressed opinions on every area, there was general agreement between them on several issues. Their attitude to the type of target language used was similar to that held by Johnstone (1995) who stated that there should be provision of undiluted forms of the language together with the teaching of grammar and error correction.

There were two main purposes behind the interviews; firstly, to explore teachers' awareness of some of the theoretical issues raised related to language teaching and, secondly, to provide information which could be further researched in the self-report sheets, the results of which are discussed in the next section.

Teachers' self-report sheets

In order to provide an additional measure of teachers' perceptions of their use of German, they were asked to complete a self-report sheet. As with the interviews, it was decided to have this done at the end of the project so that they would have time to reflect on their patterns of target language use. The self-report sheets supplemented the information obtained during the interviews and some information revealed in the interviews was incorporated into the self-report sheets. These were based on the model used in the studies by Wing (1980) and contained sixteen content areas which teachers generally carried out in the classroom. A copy of the self-report sheet can be found in Appendix B. The term 'content area' was chosen as opposed to 'function' since the latter is generally understood in its more narrow sense referring to language functions such as 'praising', 'instructing', etc. Some of the activities covered in classes, however, related more to the content of the lessons, such as 'Homework' or 'Examination techniques'.

Table 1.1   *Results of teacher self-report sheets*

Teacher	1	2	3	4	5	6	7	8	9	10	Mean
Greeting/Settling	3	4	4	3	4	3	4	1	4	2	3.2
Intro. objs	3	3	4	3	2	1	3	2	2	1	2.4
Instructions	4	3	3	4	3	1	4	2	3	3	3.0
Move from activ.	4	3	3	4	3	1	4	1	3	3	2.9
Defining vocab.	3	1	3	2	0	2	3	1	2	2	1.9
Instruc. for tests	2	0	3	1	0	1	2	0	2	0	1.1
Grammar	*	0	1	0	0	0	1	0	0	0	0.2
Exam techniques	0	0	1	0	0	0	0	0	1	0	0.2
Praising	3	4	4	4	3	3	3	2	4	4	3.4
Correcting error	3	4	2	4	2	1	2	1	3	2	2.4
Discipline	1	3	2	1	0	1	2	0	1	3	1.4
Summarising	1	2	–	3	–	0	2	1	3	0	1.2
Questions on text	2	2	3	3	3	4	3	3	3	2	2.8
Background	2	3	3	2	2	0	2	0	1	2	1.7
Homework	2	1	2	2	3	1	3	1	3	0	1.8
Personal lang.	3	3	3	4	–	1	3	2	2	3	2.4
Teacher Mean	**2.4**	**2.3**	**2.7**	**2.5**	**1.8**	**1.3**	**2.6**	**1.1**	**2.3**	**1.7**	**2.0**

*   T1 did not indicate grammar, since special extra grammar lessons are offered to pupils outwith normal school hours.

Key:	0	English 100%		3	English 25% German 75%
	1	English 75% German 25%		4	German 100%
	2	English 50% German 50%			

Teachers were asked to rank their perceived use of the target language with the project class on a scale of 0–4 to indicate the estimated percentage of target language used over a period of time. If a teacher used English 100% of the time for a particular area, for example, this would be recorded as 0 on the scale, since no German would be used for that content area. By giving the percentages of target language used as a score, it is possible to arrive at a total score for each content area and for each teacher. Thus a higher score indicates a higher use of German. The percentages for each language represent a global assessment of the proportion of time spent using each language; a teacher using the target language 75% of the time and English 25% of the time, for example, would indicate that over a period of time the target language would be used three-quarters of the time. Obviously there is a great deal of subjectivism here, since what might appear to represent 75% for one teacher might be coded as 50% for another. Furthermore, it may also depend on the time of year or the aim of particular lessons. Despite these caveats, it is interesting to gain some overall impression of the teachers' own perception of their use of German. Table 1.1 gives the summary of teachers' self-rated scores on each content area; it presents a mean score both for the teachers' overall rating of their use of German and a mean score for each of the sixteen content areas. The mean score shows the average value attached to each of the content areas and to each teacher. It is possible at a glance, therefore, to see at a glance whether an individual teacher claims to use more or less target language for a particular content area than the rest of the group.

CONTENT AREAS WITH HIGH TARGET LANGUAGE VALUES

From the mean scores it can be seen that the content areas which were rated the highest are 'Praising', 'Greeting/Settling' and 'Instructions'. It is significant that these content areas are generally only short utterances such as *'Ausgezeichnet'*, *'Guten Morgen'*, *'Macht die Bücher auf'*, so that it is hardly surprising that teachers can claim to use 100% target language for them. The diagrams presented in Appendix C illustrate the profile of each teacher on all content areas. Of interest in this group is the low score by T8 on 'Greeting/Settling'. This can be explained by his response in the interview, which stated that starting the class with *'Guten Morgen alle'*, after having spoken to pupils individually as they were entering the classroom, appeared to be a rather artificial beginning to the lesson. Both T6 and T8 maintain that they give 'Instructions' more in English than in German, which puts them at odds with the rest of the teachers who note that 'Instructions' are given in German at least 75% of the time.

CONTENT AREAS WITH AVERAGE TARGET LANGUAGE VALUES

The next group of content areas scoring mean values between 2.4 and 2.9 (therefore more than 50%), could be labelled as those with an average target language value. The top of this list is 'Moving on from activity', which, again, could be achieved by one word such as '*Also . . .*', '*Jetzt . . .*', '*OK*', described by Mitchell (1986) as discourse markers, which puts this content area in the one-word category above and is, therefore, relatively easily carried out in the target language.

The next content area, 'Questions on a text', is more difficult to interpret since it depends very much on the type of text and the purpose of the questions. If teachers are practising reading comprehensions for examination, they will invariable be using more English. Two of the teachers of the fifth form classes noted 75% German, although it might have been expected that more English would be used towards the approach of the GCSE exam. The third teacher of a fifth form, however, records only 50%. T6 gives 'Questions on a text' 100% score which is far higher than the rest of the content areas for this teacher who averages only 1.3.

'Personal language' refers to language directed personally at pupils or to a topic dealt with from their own personal point of view. For example, questions on a house would be regarded as 'Questions on a topic', but followed by questions on pupils' own homes, would be regarded as 'Personal language'. This content area was not entered by T5, which is surprising, since it would appear to be a content area which is evident in language classrooms from the very first lesson, with '*Wie heißt du?*'. The majority record this area as being carried out at least 50% of the time in the target language, which one might expect.

For 'Introducing objectives' it might have been expected that more teachers would do this in English, since it is difficult to explain to a class what they are going to do, if they do not know the vocabulary for it. However, only two teachers claimed to carry out this function more than 50% of the time in English.

CONTENT AREAS WITH LOW TARGET LANGUAGE VALUES

The remaining content areas could be said to have low target language values, with the last two, 'Grammar' and 'Examination techniques' scoring almost zero. This would conform to expectations and confirms teachers' responses in interview. For 'Giving instructions for 'Tests'', T3's score of 75% German is rather high and this might be reduced as the class progresses into fifth form. For 'Discipline', T2's score of 75% German appears high, although T10's score of 75% German is confirmed by examples in the video-recordings of disciplinary interventions being conducted in the target language.

Table 1.2   *Teacher means expressed as a percentage of target language*

Teacher	1	2	3	4	5	6	7	8	9	10	Mean
% in target language	60	57.5	67.5	62.5	42.5	32.5	65	27.5	57.5	42.5	50
Rank order			3	7	4	1	2	9 < > 5	10	6	8

From the means for each teacher, it is possible to arrive at a rank order. Table 1.2 converts the mean scores into overall percentages and lists the teachers in order. The percentage is calculated by dividing the mean score by 4 and multiplying by 100. The rank order indicates the position of teachers in relation to each other on the mean. The overall mean, based on the mean of all the content areas is taken as the dividing line between two groups of teachers, namely high and low target language users indicated by the <> signs in the rank order. It must be emphasised that these are representations of teachers' perceptions of their own target language use. A diagrammatic representation of each teacher's self-report can be found in Appendix C.

TEACHER PROFILES

In order to gain an overall picture of individual teachers' own perceptions of their use of German, the following sections will sketch an outline of each teacher's self report sheet.

Teacher 1

The areas where this teacher notes 100% use of German are 'Instructions' and 'Moving on', followed by six areas for which German is used 75% of the time, namely 'Greeting/Settling', 'Introducing objectives', 'Vocabulary', 'Praising', 'Correcting' and 'Personal language'. Equal weight is given to both languages in a further four areas, namely 'Tests', 'Questioning', 'Background' and 'Homework'. The explanation of 'Examination techniques' is usually done in English, according to this teacher. She scores herself above average for 'Introducing objectives', 'Instructions', 'Moving on', 'Vocabulary', 'Tests', 'Background' and 'Personal language'. The remaining areas are scored below the mean scores. With a mean score of 2.4, this teacher is one of the higher target language users, which is expressed as a percentage is 60%.

Teacher 2

This teacher notes three content areas where 100% target language is used, namely 'Greeting/Settling', 'Praising' and 'Correcting' with six areas in which German is used 75% such as 'Introducing objectives', 'Instructions', 'Moving on', 'Discipline', 'Background' and 'Personal language'. The only content area which might appear to have been rated comparatively highly is 'Discipline' which only one other teacher scored at this level of target language use. There are two areas where T2 notes 50% of each language, namely 'Summarising' and 'Questioning'. English is used for the larger proportion of time in 'Vocabulary' and 'Homework', with exclusive use of English for 'Tests', 'Grammar' and 'Examination techniques'. This teacher's self scores are average or above average for the majority of content areas, the exceptions being 'Vocabulary', 'Questioning', and 'Homework'. The areas where English is stated as the language of use are very slightly below the average. On balance this teacher's self-rating is above the average overall with a mean of 2.3, a percentage mean of 57.5%.

Teacher 3

This teacher notes 100% target language use for 'Greeting/Settling', 'Introducing objectives' and 'Praising', with seven areas following closely with German noted as 75%, namely 'Instructions', 'Moving on', 'Vocabulary', 'Tests', 'Background', 'Questioning' and 'Personal language'. The areas of content where 50% of each language is claimed are 'Correcting', 'Discipline' and 'Homework'. No area was rated by this teacher as being carried out 100% of the time in English, but 25% German and 75% English was estimated for 'Grammar' and 'Examination techniques'. Scoring above average on all except one of the completed categories, 'Correcting', this teacher is rated the highest target language user according to self-ratings with a mean of 2.7 which, as a percentage, is 67.5% .

Teacher 4

This teacher notes five areas where German is used 100% of the time, namely 'Instructions', 'Moving on', 'Praising', 'Correcting' and 'Personal language', which represents more areas with 100% target language than all the other teachers. 'Greeting/Settling' along with 'Introducing', 'Summarising' and 'Questioning' score 75% German. Both languages are indicated as equal for 'Vocabulary', 'Background' and 'Homework', with 'Tests', and 'Discipline' using more English than German and the two areas of 'Grammar' and 'Examination techniques' done exclusively in English. This teacher scores above average on 'Introducing objectives', 'Instructions', 'Moving on', 'Vocabulary', 'Praising', 'Correcting', 'Background', 'Summarising', 'Questioning', 'Homework' and 'Personal language'. With a mean score of 2.5, T4 is one of the highest users of the target language, according to self evaluation which is 62.5%.

Teacher 5

Only one area is noted as being done 100% in the target language by this teacher, namely 'Greeting/Settling'. At the other end of the scale, five areas are done entirely in English, namely 'Vocabulary', 'Tests', 'Grammar', 'Examination techniques' and 'Discipline'. Scoring 75% for German are 'Instructions', 'Moving on', 'Praising', 'Questioning' and 'Homework' with a 50% score for 'Introducing objectives', 'Correcting' and 'Background'. Two of the areas were omitted by this teacher, namely 'Summarising' and 'Personal language'. This teacher is one of the three fifth form teachers, which may explain a relatively high English score. Scoring average or just above average scores on only five areas, this teacher remains, with 1.8 personal average, below the mean at 42.5%.

Teacher 6

This teacher notes a relatively high score for English on all of the topic areas except 'Questioning'. Those indicated as being done 100% in English are 'Grammar', 'Examination techniques', 'Summarising' and 'Background', with 'Introducing objectives', 'Instructions', 'Moving on', 'Tests', 'Correcting', 'Discipline', 'Homework' and 'Personal language' as 75% English. The relatively easy areas to carry out in the target language, such as 'Greeting/Settling' and 'Praising', receive a score of 75% German. All of the scores, with the exception of 'Vocabulary' and 'Questioning', are below the average score and 'Vocabulary' is only 0.1 above the average. It is noteworthy that this teacher is the only one to note 100% target language for 'Questioning'. With these self-noted scores, T6 is rated as having an average score of 1.3 which as a percentage is 32.5% and thus is well below the mean score overall. When presented with these findings, the only teacher who was surprised at the overall score was T6 who was convinced that she used the target language on average 60% of the time.

Teacher 7

Three content areas are noted by this teacher as being conducted 100% in the target language, namely 'Greeting/Settling', 'Instructions' and 'Moving on'. Several others are recorded as being carried out 75% in the target language: 'Introducing objectives', 'Vocabulary', 'Praising', 'Questioning', 'Homework' and 'Personal language'. The areas which are noted as being carried out 50% in each language are 'Tests', 'Correcting', 'Background', 'Discipline' and 'Summarising'. Only two areas are listed as being done significantly in English: 'Grammar' (25% in the target language) and 'Examination techniques' (English 100% of the time). Only three of the scores noted by T7 are below the average, namely 'Examination techniques', 'Praising' and 'Correcting', which results in his attaining an overall above average score of 2.6 and, as such, he is the second highest target language user according to self-evaluation with 65%.

Teacher 8

This teacher has a similar profile to that of T6, with the majority of content areas weighted more to English than to German. Five areas are coded as being conducted 100% in English: 'Tests', 'Grammar', 'Examination techniques', 'Discipline' and 'Background', with six areas 75% of the time in English: 'Greeting/Settling', 'Moving on', 'Vocabulary', 'Correcting', 'Summarising' and 'Homework'. The remainder are 50% in English, with the exceptions of 'Questioning' which has 75% target language value. This is similar to the relatively higher value attributed to this area by T6. With this area as the only exception, all others are below the average value, resulting in T8's lowest position on the use of the target language according to self evaluation with an average of 1.1 which is only 27.5%.

Teacher 9

Two areas are noted by T9 as being carried out 100% of the time in German, namely 'Greeting/Settling' and 'Praising', which have been noted as two of the easiest content areas to conduct in the target language. Six areas follow with a value of 75%: 'Instructions', 'Moving on', 'Correcting', 'Summarising', 'Questioning' and 'Homework'. The four areas of 'Introducing objectives', 'Vocabulary', 'Tests' and 'Personal language' are coded as 50% in each language. Three others are done 75% of the time in English: 'Examination techniques', 'Discipline' and 'Background', with 'Grammar' being the only one taught 100% in English. Some areas are just above the average score, namely 'Moving on' and 'Vocabulary', with 'Instructions' on the mean with a score of 75%. Others which are above the mean are: 'Greeting/Settling', 'Tests', 'Examination techniques', 'Praising', 'Correcting', 'Summarising', 'Questions on text' and 'Homework'. The five remaining areas, namely 'Introducing objectives', 'Grammar', 'Background', 'Discipline' and 'Personal language', have values slightly below the mean. Overall, however, T9 has a mean score of 2.3 which puts her above the general mean with a percentage of 57.5%, the same average as T2.

Teacher 10

The last teacher only notes one area where German is used 100% of the time, namely 'Praising'. Four areas are noted as being conducted in German 75% of the time, namely 'Instructions', 'Moving on', 'Discipline' and 'Personal language'. The areas of 'Greeting/Settling', 'Vocabulary', 'Correcting', 'Questions on a text' and 'Background' are noted as being done 50% in each language, with 'Introducing objectives' being conducted 75% of the time in English. Five remaining areas, namely 'Tests', 'Grammar', 'Examination techniques', 'Summarising' and 'Homework', are all done 100% of the time in English. Of the sixteen noted content areas, this teacher scores one on the mean, two marginally above the mean by 0.1, four above and the remainder below. With an overall average score of 1.7 this teacher is coded as below the overall mean score with 42.5%.

SUMMARY

From the self ratings of the teachers, four are noted as scoring themselves above the average, namely T3, T7, T4 and T1, with two significantly below, T6 and T8, and the remainder clustering round the mean, two just above, T2 and T9, and two below, T5 and T10. It must be reiterated, however, that these are the teachers' perceptions of their own practice in areas, many of which teachers may not consciously have in their lesson schemes and consequently may have misrepresented. They provide some indication of how teachers view their practice. From both the interviews and the teacher self-report questionnaire, it appears that all teachers in the sample are convinced, on the basis of experience, of the benefits of sustained although not exclusive use of the target language. This agrees with the findings of Mitchell (1988) and Franklin (1990) and with the literature which indicates that a balance of languages is appropriate (e.g. Buckby, 1985; Atkinson, 1993).

The analysis of the interviews and the self-report sheets taken together suggests that teachers differentiate between the various content areas of the language lesson and that the balance of German and English differs depending on the content area. This in many ways mirrors the findings of Wing (1980), Mitchell (1988) and Franklin (1990) who identified a hierarchy of areas with the straightforward ones, such as 'Greeting', 'Praising', 'Instructions', 'Organising the class' much more easily conducted in the target language than those at the other end such as 'Grammar', 'Discipline', 'Examination techniques'. Hamilton (1994) states that these more difficult areas are those which have been neglected in in-service training. Some areas differed from the early studies, however, such as the teaching of 'Background' and 'Introducing objectives', which teachers in Mitchell's (1988) study suggested would be better done in English. Communicative language teaching has moved on since the days of Wing (1980) and Mitchell (1986, 1988); and teachers are now more confident in their use of the target language and are more convinced that what they are doing is right.

CONCLUSION

The teacher data as revealed in the interview and self-report sheets have been discussed in this chapter. This is the first stage in arriving at a detailed analysis of the German used in the classroom. The following chapter considers the subject from the pupils' point of view and makes some comparisons between teachers' and pupils' views.

Chapter 2

Pupil perspectives

In order to gain a different perspective on each teacher's use of German, a sample of pupils in each class was interviewed. The information gained from the three pupils from each class was incorporated in a follow-up questionnaire which was given to all pupils in each of the project classes. The first part of this chapter presents the findings of the interviews and the second part gives details of the pupils' responses to the questionnaire.

Pupils' interviews

In the pupil interviews the topics investigated were as follows:

1 views on German in general;
2 difficulties in learning German;
3 target language input;
4 use of English;
5 the most important skill;
6 opportunities for output and interaction;
7 communicative competence and confidence;
8 the role of grammar;
9 the role of error correction.

Since the interviews were conducted with groups of three pupils, their responses will be presented as a group response. The pupils of the project teachers will be identified by the same letter as the teacher, for example P1 to represent the group of pupils interviewed from T1's class.

DOMAIN 1   VIEWS ON GERMAN

Before focusing specifically on teachers' use of German in the classroom, pupils were asked their views on German as a language. They were asked why they had chosen to continue learning German at Key Stage 4 and in particular which aspects they found appealing. The answers to these questions clustered around two main reasons. The first related to the pupils' general interest in the subject in the initial years, which was linked in each case to different factors, such as their liking for the teacher, their preference for the sound of the language or past experience with the country through family contacts. The second main reason offered was related to the utilitarian value of the language, which was elaborated in some instances to mention Germany's important place in the EU as the largest country or in more general terms to mention the value of the language in finding employment.

Some pupils simply stated that they **had** to choose one language and, faced with the choice of German or Spanish, they chose German (P6). Others commented that since it was not a compulsory subject, they were more motivated to work hard at it and do well in it (P4). Enthusiasm for the subject was expressed by all of the P1 group who almost said in unison: '*German is just what you want to do*'. Apart from the nature of the work done in their German class, this was attributed to the very pleasant atmosphere in the classroom created by their teacher's infectious enthusiasm for the subject.

DOMAIN 2   DIFFICULTIES IN LEARNING GERMAN

The question which followed was designed to explore aspects which pupils found difficult and, in cases where pupils were learning more than one language, they were asked to compare their views on German with the other language (in most cases French). Two groups of pupils said that they found German a difficult language but stated that they regarded it as a challenge. Others thought that it was more like English than French and these pupils had decided to drop French in favour of German. One male pupil found the pronunciation of German more desirable than French because:

> . . . *you could speak German naturally without having to force some kind of artificial accent.* (P5)

On the other hand, having an ability at French was the reason why several pupils wanted to continue with more than one language (P1, P2, P7, P9).

Several pupils compared German with French and commented more favourably on German because of the following features: the sound of the language; the relative ease of pronunciation; the logical nature of the syntax; the regularity of verbs (one pupil mentioned the similarity of the infinitives, another the tenses) and the large number of cognates. One pupil mentioned that German was easier in the initial stages, but that it became progressively more difficult. Only one female pupil preferred French, saying that it flowed more easily than German. One fourth form pupil was conscious that she had been learning French for longer and commented that she would do better in the GCSE French examination because of the extra time available.

The difficulties of the language might have been predicted, but it was important that the thoughts came from the pupils themselves. No attempt was made to prompt pupils, since this might have changed their perceptions. One pupil, for example, mentioned German word order as much simpler, whereas this was mentioned by other groups of pupils as a major source of difficulty. The general term 'grammar' was used by different pupils to mean different things . Examples given were the case system, genders, endings, word order and compound words. As the fourth form pupils had been concentrating on adjective endings around the time of the interviews, many of them commented on this particular aspect of the grammar as an area of specific difficulty. None of the pupils regarded these difficulties either as impediments to enjoyment or to eventual attainment in German.

This area was important to examine because the pupils' views on the language in general may influence their perception of their teachers' use of German in the classroom.

DOMAIN 3   TARGET LANGUAGE INPUT

This part of the interview dealt with two related issues, namely the target language produced by the teacher and the access pupils had to other sources of target language input, either within the classroom or outside school.

When asked about the amount of German used by their teachers, all of the groups were convinced that their teacher used the foreign language enough in the class. The pupils of T6 commented that, although they perceived their teacher to use German only 25% of the time, they felt that was sufficient and that they would not be able to cope with any more.

A further issue was explored, namely the strategies employed by teachers when the pupils did not understand something in the target language. Some interesting techniques had been noticed by pupils:

> [The teacher] will use another word in German that sounds like the English. (P1)
> She speaks more slowly and clearly. (P1)
> If we don't understand, sometimes the teacher will write it on the board. (P1)
> The teacher will just say it in English or we'd get lost. (P5)
> By [the teacher's] using facial expressions and actions, we can work it out. (P4)
> Another person in the class translates for the rest. (P2)
> [He] would emphasise a part of the word which we knew, or would say it in a different way or a different tone. (P7)
> He uses lots of hand signals to make the meaning clear. (P8)

This last group was asked whether they would prefer to hear the English to make something clear, as this would save time. They unanimously responded that they would prefer the hand signals, because by hearing they would improve and would know what it meant the next time. What is interesting in the answers above is that the pupils seemed to be completely aware of the fact that their teachers were making an effort to make the language comprehensible for them and they clearly identified what might be regarded as good practice strategies, namely:

- use of cognates;
- slower delivery;
- clearer speech, change of tone;
- written support;
- mime and gesture;
- use of a class interpreter;
- decoding into English as a last resort.

A related issue referred to the provision of German within the classroom, either by a foreign language assistant or by cassettes and/or video. The presence of a foreign language assistant was welcomed by most pupils, although they had some thoughts on the differences between a native and a non-native-speaker of German. Whilst it was admitted that they were learning the language in order to be able to communicate with real Germans, many of them preferred to have a non-native speaker as a teacher. The accent of a native-speaker was thought to cause difficulty and the overuse of idioms was regarded as a disadvantage. One pupil captured the essence of many of the groups' thoughts:

> *A native-speaker has advantages in that he or she knows the language and can teach you more slang. But a non-native-speaker knows the difficulties of the language. Where it is a person's first language, they do not make allowances for you because they don't know the difficulties. English would be difficult for me to teach because I don't know the grammar.* (P7)

The foreign language assistant was different because he or she mainly took conversation classes, although the collaborative team-teaching which was a major feature in T1's classes was appreciated by the pupils. In addition to this, pupils in this class were given extra classes with the foreign language assistant. One commented:

> *Speaking German with [the assistant], you just don't realise you are learning.* (P1)

All pupils agreed that the tapes were far less intelligible than either the teachers or the foreign language assistants because of the speed, the quality of the recording and the general background noise. This raises the issue of the value of providing language which is taken from authentic contexts but used in the artificial environment of the foreign language classroom. The point was made by these pupils:

> *When you are in the real-life situation you can read the person's lips and ask for repetition, but the voice on tape is much more difficult to understand.* (P1)

Some other pupils pointed out that the listening comprehensions done in class were only comprehensible because the pupils had to listen for specific items of information. Extended language without guidelines would be very difficult to understand. A hint of Krashen's requirements of comprehensible input such as extralinguistic cues and context was mentioned:

> [. . .] if you are to have a vague idea of what is being said, you have to know a bit about the context. (P2)

Teachers were able to make the language much more comprehensible because of their ability to respond to cues from pupils, because of their knowledge of the context and because they could adjust the language by using simplification strategies.

Only very few pupils had access to other sources of input. One girl (P7) took singing lessons and found many of the texts in German added to her vocabulary. Satellite television was available in some schools and some pupils had access to it at home, although they did not appear to be in a position, yet, to take advantage of this undiluted form of input.

DOMAIN 4   USE OF ENGLISH

Apart from grammar, most pupils agreed that the main areas of the work were carried out, at least to some degree, in the target language, with the exception of examination practice (P8), in particular for reading and listening comprehensions which are tested in English. The pupils in T1's class were the only ones to mention that homework was explained in German and then repeated in English, which confirms this teacher's self rating of 50% for both languages on this activity described in the previous chapter. Although there would be occasions when English is used spontaneously, pupils appeared to be convinced that they were being exposed to German in various contexts within the classroom.

DOMAIN 5   THE MOST IMPORTANT SKILL

Differing views were expressed on this point with various differences of opinion occurring between groups of pupils and between individuals within groups. Some saw the most important outcome of the German course as the ability to speak when they went to the target country. One girl (P10) commented, however, that many pupils would not get to Germany and, even if they did, they would be more likely to write beforehand, so that writing was more important than speaking. Another group (P6) stated that writing was the most important skill because you needed to know the grammar and vocabulary in order to write, so that if you could write well, you would be able to speak, listen and read. The pupils who preferred writing stated that this was because they liked writing in English and they wrote lots of letters. One pupil (P8) pointed to a difference between speaking and writing: 'in writing you have more time to think and to *get it right'.* In so saying she echoed the thoughts of Krashen who stated that, in order to focus on the rules to monitor performance, time is necessary.

A combination of speaking and listening was mentioned by several, although one group (P10) all agreed that listening was the most important because speaking would follow. One boy, who had been in Germany, remarked that it was important to be able to speak since *'the Germans appreciate your trying to speak'.* (P8)

Reading was not mentioned by many groups, but one girl, echoing the thoughts of many teachers, said:

> I think reading is a bit neglected. There should be more reading, especially for the exams. (P3)

Presumably all the pupils interviewed expressed, to a certain extent, the opinions of their teachers or reflected the types of skills which are either frequently practised or which are perceived by them to be neglected in the syllabus.

DOMAIN 6 OPPORTUNITIES FOR OUTPUT AND INTERACTION

All of the groups interviewed mentioned a variety of activities done in class which were based on all four skill areas. All of the pupils felt that it was important to do pairwork as it gave them the opportunity to practise structures learned and to talk to each other in German. Role plays were mentioned by all of the groups, since this was a frequent activity in most classes observed. One pupil highlighted particular types of role plays as enjoyable:

> I prefer the role plays where we can make up our own versions. You can get words for yourself, so that you can build up a personal list. [You can get the words] from the teacher or from the dictionary or from the listening comprehensions, although that is a bit more difficult. (P7)

This mention of independent and creative work by pupils was perhaps significantly the only one, which suggests that far from creating independent learners of the language, the original GCSE syllabus forces teachers into providing opportunities for controlled practice only and at the pre-communicative stage.

It was unanimously felt that communicating with the foreign language assistant was an important aspect of classroom activities, in that extra help with pronunciation was available.

Group work, individualised learning and a carousel of activities were mentioned by only one group (P5). This type of work was thought to be interesting, varied and above all useful, in that it enabled the teacher to work with small groups for oral work. As this was a GCSE class in fifth form, two months before the exam, they appreciated this type of attention, although it appeared that this had been a regular feature of T5's lessons during the past two years.

One of the priorities in recent documents, as mentioned in the introduction (see p4), is the notion that pupils should be using the target language spontaneously. One area within the classroom where this might be possible is in asking for help in the target language, especially when the teacher has said something in German which the pupils have not understood. The pupils mentioned various ways the teachers encouraged them to use German, such as being given lists of set phrases which they might need, or notices displayed around the classroom. One pupil (P3) commented that the teacher always insisted on the use of the target language by pupils for certain things such as 'Wie sagt man . . ?', 'Wie schreibt man', 'Ich verstehe nicht'. Teacher consistency was seen as important, since the pupils knew the rules and they had the linguistic resources to present their requests.

DOMAIN 7   COMMUNICATIVE COMPETENCE AND CONFIDENCE

The question regarding the extent to which pupils felt that they could function outside the classroom environment led on naturally from comments made in the previous question. The general gist of the answers was that most pupils felt that they could cope, but several added that they were only able to cope within the confines of the topic areas which appeared in the textbook. One pupil commented:

> I would not like to have to stay with a German family because there would be a lot of conversations I wouldn't understand. I wouldn't like to be faced with a situation where the Germans were speaking and I was understanding nothing. (P9)

It seems rather surprising that a communicative approach which is designed to prepare the pupils for real-life situations should be perceived by pupils to be a tourist-type course, equipping them only for transactional situations:

> I would be able to do the basic things such as directions, and would be able to be polite, but I would not be able to have an extended conversation. (P9)

> When in Germany I was in situations not covered in the books and I was totally lost, although in other situations covered in the books I can go in and ramble on. (P8)

Another group, commenting on the transactional situations, said that they get confused because all the situations seemed the same. This comment was made by several pupils concerning their ability to function independently of the course book in the target country. The impression was given by the pupils that they are being trained for communicative competence within the confines of the GCSE examination and able to function well in those set situations. In situations which may be more interesting to them, however, they are at a loss, because they do not possess the grammatical competence nor the strategic competence needed to succeed. One might also question the justification of spending five years teaching pupils a language in which they can only perform such a limited repertoire of tasks in a limited range of situations.

From the comments of pupils in this and the previous section, it appears that they are not being taught as communicatively as teachers and inspectors might be led to believe.

DOMAIN 8 THE ROLE OF GRAMMAR

Grammar was thought to be important by all the pupils interviewed, although they stated that it was not the most important aspect of the work, and that you could get by without knowing too much grammar. Some pupils developed their answers to give details of how the grammar was taught, namely that the teacher gave examples, they practised the examples, the rule was explained and then they were given a grammar note (P3). This confirms this particular teacher's method as explained in the interview with T3 and it was reflected in video-recorded lessons. One group consisted of two pupils who studied Latin (P2), both of whom were less than satisfied with the teaching approach in French and German classrooms:

> *In German there are no grammar notes like in Latin, so we have*
> *to try and remember from the phrases we learned.* (P2)

Grammar was also thought to be important by the P7 group, one of whom has already been quoted on the aspect of being creative in the role play situation. One group protested that they did not have the necessary basis in the language to be creative, and that they were only capable of learning rote phrases from the book:

> *For example in phrases like* **'Haben Sie noch Plätze frei?'** *I*
> *couldn't use another phrase like it because I don't know what*
> **noch** *means.* (P2)

This was a common complaint made by the interviewed pupils. It appears then, by comparing the answers in this section with those in the previous domain, that the teaching of German for these pupils is neither exclusively communicative nor purely grammar-based, but that it is what might be described as a healthy combination, consisting of elements of both traditions in an eclectic approach. Despite this, however, the pupils feel that they do not have enough communicative German to converse with confidence in more than a restricted number of situations, nor do they have enough grammatical awareness in order to be linguistically independent.

DOMAIN 9 THE ROLE OF ERROR CORRECTION

When asked about the need for accuracy and the need to be corrected by the teacher, the main response was that the most important thing was to get the meaning across and mistakes were not serious as long as comprehension was not impeded. In giving this answer, the pupils were merely repeating their teachers' views on how to pass the GCSE exam. However, one group saw rewards in being accurate:

> [Accuracy] is not essential, but it made you feel good when we were in Berlin and the people understood. It made me like it all the more. Conveying the message is the main thing, but you like to get it right because you know you are doing something right. (P1)

All of the pupils saw the need to be corrected but not at the expense of communication.

In the two sections above, namely grammar and error correction, there is a great deal of similarity between the pupils' views and the teachers' own views of their practice, which suggests that the pupils were expressing not their own beliefs, but rather their subconscious awareness of what was happening in their German lessons. This is a feature which is difficult to disentangle and one which emerges in the questionnaires, namely the difficulty in discerning whether the pupils are expressing their own views or are stating what is the case at the moment in their lessons.

SUMMARY OF INTERVIEWS

From the interviews with the various groups of pupils it emerged that they appeared to have a fairly clear idea of what went on in their linguistic environment, in particular, they had views on the type of target language provided, on the opportunities afforded them to use the language and they had some awareness of their own communicative limitations in German.

Pupil questionnaires

Several of the responses made during the interviews were incorporated into the questionnaires for pupils which was based on the model used by Duff and Polio (1990). A copy of the adapted version can be found in Appendix D. The first two sections are relevant to the teachers' use of the target language, namely:

- Pupil details
- Pupil perceptions of teacher target language use.

PUPIL DETAILS

Out of a possible 200 pupils, there were 184 responses which are detailed in Table 2.1.

Table 2.1   *Details of pupils responding*

School/Teacher code										
	1	2	3	4	5	6	7	8	9	10	Total
Form	5	4	4	4	5	4	4	5	4	4	–
Pupils	17	24	17	28	18	17	26	20	21	12	200
Replies	15	24	16	26	17	16	23	18	19	10	184
Absent	2	0	1	2	1	1	3	2	2	2	16

The vast majority (100 pupils) was learning both German and French; German was the sole language of 74 of the pupils and the remaining ten were learning Latin in addition to German and French.

PUPIL PERCEPTIONS

This section of the questionnaire divided up the lesson into six content areas which could be identified by the pupils. Most of the areas are self-explanatory, such as 'Grammar', 'Homework', 'Discipline' and 'Background'. Two areas require some explanation, since they are fairly similar:

- 'Instructions for activity' — when the teacher uses language to set up an activity.
- 'Classroom language' — instructions such as 'take out your books'; 'pack up', etc.

The pupils were asked to state which language the teacher used, either German or English; where teachers used both languages this was to be indicated by putting a tick in both columns.

Responses to this question will first be presented in summary form and by individual teacher in Appendix E.

Table 2.2   *Pupil perception of teacher target language use —*
summary data

Questions 5–10: When your teacher does the following things in class, does he or she use English or German?

% of all pupils indicating:

Content area	English	German	Both	No
Instructions for activity	11.4	62.5	26.1	
Grammar	81.0	4.9	14.1	
Giving homework	35.9	39.1	25.0	
Background	47.8	23.9	27.2	(1.1)
Classroom language	8.2	82.1	9.2	(0.5)
Discipline	54.9	25.5	17.9	(1.6)

The interesting points to note in this table are, first, the high percentage of pupils who ticked German for the language of 'Classroom language', and the high number stating that the 'Grammar' was generally conducted through English. Furthermore, more than half the pupils noted that 'Instructions for activity' were given in German and that 'Discipline' was carried out in English. This would concur with the findings from both interviews and from the teacher questionnaires. In order to give an individual breakdown by teacher, Appendix E presents the findings of pupils for each teacher.

The results in Appendix E are different from those in Appendix C (the teachers perceptions of their own practice), although both sets are presented as percentages. In the teachers' perception of their own practice (Appendix C) the percentages represent the estimated time that the teacher conducted the content areas in German or English. The results of the pupil questionnaires when presented as percentages, however, (Appendix E) represent the total number of pupils who indicated a particular language. For example, since all the fifteen pupils in the class of T1 noted that this teacher used German when giving 'Instructions for activity' and 'Classroom language', these areas are scored as 100%. What the pupil results tell us, therefore, is the extent to which the teacher is perceived to be using German or English by his or her class.

It can be seen from the diagrams in Appendix E that there is a fairly high level of agreement between respondents for each teacher, especially the pupils of T1 and T6 on three content areas, T3 and T10 on two and T7 on one. Initial results from this aspect of the study were presented elsewhere (Neil, 1996).

T1 is seen by 100% of her pupils to use German for 'Instructions for activity' and 'Classroom language' (as is T3 and T10) and to use English for 'Grammar. T6 is viewed by her pupils to use predominantly English for all of the areas. This appears to suggest that these teachers are so consistent in carrying out these particular content areas in one of the languages that the pupils are in no doubt as to what to what language is used for that area of the work.

Where the pupils indicate that both languages are used, this may mean either that the teachers use different languages depending on the context of the lesson, or that they use both languages (i.e. that either they code-switch or that they decode); the questionnaire was not sufficiently refined to differentiate in this respect.

The following three questions in the questionnaire provided summative data asking the pupils to think in general terms about their teachers' use of German in the classroom.

Table 2.3   *Q11 — How much German does your teacher use in class?*

	% of pupils responding									
Teacher	**1**	**2**	**3**	**4**	**5**	**6**	**7**	**8**	**9**	**10**
A lot	100	70.8	100	80.0	52.9	25	95.7	50	89.5	100
Some		29.2		19.2	47.1	50	4.3	50	10.5	
Little					25					

Although terms such as 'A lot' (most of the time) could be interpreted differently by classes and by individuals in one class, there appears to be consistency between this table and the pupils' perception of individual areas of lessons (refer again to Appendix E). It is significant also that three of the teachers who were ranked highest in their own perception of their use of the target language (see Table 1.2) were T1, T3 and T7 who came in the top four in the pupils' view. Furthermore, T6 and T8 came out as the lowest target language users in both cases.

A further measure of internal consistency can be confirmed by the next question which asked the pupils how much they would like their teacher to use, compared to what they experience at the moment. Table 2.4 presents the responses in terms of 'More', 'Same' or 'Less' than at present.

Table 2.4   *Q12 — How much German would you like your teacher to use in class?*

	% of pupils responding									
Teacher	**1**	**2**	**3**	**4**	**5**	**6**	**7**	**8**	**9**	**10**
More		4.2				31.3		11.1		
Same	93.3	75	93.8	96.2	52.9	68.8	47.8	88.9	89.5	50
Less	6.7	20.8	6.3	3.8	47.1		52.2		10.5	50

These results seem to confirm that pupils have been more or less consistent throughout the questionnaire, since none of the four top scoring teachers' pupils want more than now, whereas the two consistently lowest scoring teachers have pupils who want more German than at present and the majority are content with what is offered. As was pointed out earlier, it is difficult to make generalisations on this, since pupils can only talk about what they are used to and find it difficult to hypothesise as to what implications more German spoken in the classroom might have.

The final summative question asked pupils to reflect on how much they understood of the teachers' German. The results to this question are important since, if one of the prerequisites of using the target language in the class is to ensure that the input is comprehensible, high percentages in the lower categories of 'Some' and 'Very little' would give cause for concern.

Table 2.5   Q13 — *How much of what the teacher says in German do you understand?*

% of pupils responding										
Teacher	1	2	3	4	5	6	7	8	9	10
All of it			6.3			6.3	4.3			
Most	93.3	45.8	81.3	92.3	29.4	68.8	65.2	72.2	84.2	50
Some	6.7	54.2	12.5	7.7	41.2	25	26.1	16.7	15.8	40
Very little					29.4		4.3	11.1		10

It is gratifying that most of the respondents tick that they understood at least 'Some' of the German directed at them, with very high percentages of the pupils of T1, T3, T4 and T9 noting that they understand most of it. The percentages in the last row 'Very little' represent five pupils of T5, two of T8 and one each of T7 and T10. One might have expected more of the pupils of teachers who are perceived to use less of the target language, such as T6, to indicate that they understand 'All of it'. The fact that two pupils of T8 (11.1%) stated they understood 'Very little' is perhaps rather alarming for fifth formers about to take GCSE exams.

SUMMARY

Since there has been very little written about pupils' perceptions of their teachers' use of the target language, it is not possible to relate the findings of this chapter to any previous study.

It would appear that the pupils in the study have fairly well-formed views on their preferences in learning German; their responses both in interviews and in the questionnaires reveal that they appear to have thought out some of the issues, suggested by the consistency which was evident both between the interviews and the questionnaires and between the specific and more general sections of the questionnaire.

The pupils appeared to be relatively satisfied with the balance of activities offered in their classrooms, although some expressed reservations about the balance of skill areas. The data from the pupil interviews confirmed the suspicions of teachers and the sentiments of Edmunds (1995) that the communicative approach has led to a reduction in linguistic independence and creativity for pupils. The pupils were also very aware of the importance of conveying meaning as opposed simply to knowing the form, views which were based largely on their experience of being taught communicatively, but also influenced by the emphasis of the forthcoming GCSE examination. Some of the pupils appeared to realise that although error correction was not necessary in order to convey meaning, it was essential if they were to improve and, for one pupil, to know she was getting it right enhanced her linguistic self-esteem.

It was also interesting that the pupils had some idea of the simplification strategies used by their teachers and that they were able to identify the extra-linguistic cues employed by teachers to convey meaning. They were also able to comment on the advantages and disadvantages of having a native speaker as opposed to a non-native speaker as a teacher and were able to compare and contrast the linguistic input provided by the foreign language assistant with the authentic material produced on tape.

With regard to the teachers' use of German, the perceptions of some groups of pupils, when considered as a unit, are fairly similar to the views expressed by the teachers. The pupils seemed aware of the languages which were being used by the teachers for the various content areas, except in circumstances where the teachers were perhaps inconsistent in their choice of language.

The teachers were given an overview of their pupils' responses and many were interested to find the correlation between their own views and the perceptions of their pupils. Some took the responses in the final section as a justification for continuing with their present quantity of target language. The question remains, however, as to the extent to which the teachers and pupils present accurate pictures of what actually happens in the German classes.

Chapter 3

Observed lessons

The previous two chapters have examined the use of German in the classroom at Key Stage 4 from two perspectives; first, the teachers' perceptions of their own practice and, secondly, the pupils' thoughts on their teachers' use of the language. This chapter presents findings from a third approach, namely classroom observation, and from a third perspective, that of the independent researcher.

COLLECTING THE DATA

The teachers agreed to be video-taped ten times during the first and second terms. Since the length of lessons differed from school to school, the total number of minutes recorded was restricted to 400 (i.e. ten lessons of 40 minutes). The researcher video-recorded the lessons, but did not participate in them. Although it is impossible for the presence of a camera not to influence the conduct of the lesson, it appeared that the teachers and the pupils got used to it after two or three recordings.

ANALYSING THE DATA

One of the problems encountered at the analysis stage in this study was the vast amount of data collected; to analyse 400 minutes of lesson time was impractical for one part-time researcher, so that the total lesson time analysed for each teacher was restricted to 120 minutes. The advantage of this was that flexibility was allowed in the lessons selected for analysis and it meant that all lengths of lessons could be accommodated (e.g. six lessons at 20 minutes; four at 30 minutes, three at 40 minutes). Two stages were involved in the analysis process:

- *Stage 1 — Timed analysis* was an attempt to find out the quantity of German compared to English used by the teachers.
- *Stage 2 — Content area analysis* was carried out on transcripts of the video-recorded lessons in order to see if there was any relationship between what the teachers said they did in class and what was captured on the video.

Quantity of target language

The timed analysis used to quantify the amount of German spoken and by whom was carried out by noting every ten seconds which party was speaking (either the teacher or a pupil) and the language which was being used. The 120 minutes for each teacher, when divided by ten seconds, resulted in 720 possible segments which could be coded according to the following categories:

- teacher target language;
- teacher mother tongue;
- foreign language assistant target language;
- pupil target language;
- pupil mother tongue;
- pairwork/group work;
- silence/writing/reading.

By totalling the number of ticks in each of the above categories, it was possible to arrive at a picture of what the balance was for each teacher between teacher talk and pupil talk and between the teachers' use of German and English. Table 3.1.1 below shows the percentage of teacher talk which was in the target language and that which was in English. The difference between the total and 100% can be explained by instances where the teacher was either reading aloud in the target language or translating utterances verbatim into English (which was a major feature of the lessons of T6).

Table 3.1.1   Teacher talk

Teacher	1	2	3	4	5	6	7	8	9	10
German	83.6	79.3	95.8	77.6	86.5	33.1	97.5	62.2	87.6	54.8
English	16.3	19.8	0.8	21.4	10.2	38.5	2.2	35.5	9.9	42.8
Total	99.9	99.1	96.6	99.0	96.7	71.6	99.7	97.7	97.5	97.6

A comparison of this table with the findings in chapters 1 and 2 reveals that teachers T3 and T7, the highest target language users on the observation data, were also the highest according to their own views and the perceptions of their pupils and that T6 is the lowest user of German on all three counts. There appears to be consistency, therefore, on all three measures at the top of the scale and at the bottom. This table does not take account of the many other features which were involved in the lessons, however, such as group work, use of the tape-recorder, pupil talk and paired activities. The following table (Table 3.1.2) shows the amount of time the teacher spent speaking overall, expressed as a percentage of the whole lesson time.

Table 3.1.2   Teacher talk as % of lesson

Teacher	1*	2	3	4	5	6	7	8	9	10
% of talk	64.4	55.2	50.1	54.6	47.5	54.2	44.3	47.4	60.4	76.8

* includes FLA talk

This table shows that the teacher who spoke most in lessons was T10, followed by T1, whose time was shared with the foreign language assistant. Of the high target language users, T3 spoke more overall than did T7. The lowest target language user, T6, spent a considerable amount of time talking, most of which was done in English.

Although the main focus of this book is on the teachers' use of the target language, it is interesting, in addition, to look at the time spent by the pupils talking. Table 3.2.1 shows the amount of pupil talk in German and in English. In calculating the amount of pupil talk, the times when pairwork was being done is included, but group work is excluded. Where the scores do not add up to 100% this can be explained by instances of pupils reading aloud, which were excluded from the final total.

Table 3.2.1   Pupil talk

Pupils	1	2	3	4	5	6	7	8	9	10
German	87.0	75.6	97.3	79.0	86.8	42.3	86.2	82.8	93.5	66.1
English	10.7	23.9	2.7	18.9	0	8.0	3.7	0.5	6.4	33.9
Total	97.7	99.5	100	97.9	86.8	50.3	89.9	83.3	99.9	100

It is encouraging to notice the high percentage of German used by the pupils, but this requires further clarification. The percentages indicate the global amount of time given to pupil talk as a class and not the amount of time given to each individual pupil. If the amount of time devoted to pupil talk is expressed as a percentage of the lesson as a whole, a rather more worrying picture is presented.

Table 3.2.2   Pupil talk as % of lesson

Pupils	1	2	3	4	5	6	7	8	9	10
% of talk	18.1	24.4	25.8	21.3	16.8	24.3	26.1	25.8	12.9	7.8

This table confirms the fears expressed by inspectors that pupils are not given sufficient opportunities to use the target language. All teachers, when shown these figures, were very surprised at the lack of pupil involvement as they appeared unaware of the one-sided nature of many of their lessons. As stated above, these figures are global figures for each class. If this percentage of pupil talk in German is divided by the number of pupils in the class, in order to arrive at an overall average number of minutes over the 120-minute analysed time, the following emerges:

Table 3.2.3   Average number of minutes of pupil target language

Pupils	1	2	3	4	5	6	7	8	9	10
Mins per pupil	1.0	0.9	1.8	0.7	0.9	0.7	1.0	1.3	0.7	0.5

The fact that an average pupil would be speaking German for a maximum of two minutes every two hours is something which should be of concern to language teachers and it is an issue which requires some attention. Obviously, the provision of paired activities do little to increase the time which pupils speak in the target language. Nor indeed does group work appear to be the solution, since much of the time in group work tasks is spent discussing the task in English. The problem will be one of the priorities which will have to be addressed in the next few years of language teaching.

Content area analysis

At this stage of the analysis, the transcripts of the 120 minutes' lesson time recorded for each teacher were divided into the various units, according to the focus of activity. It must be emphasised that the content analysed and the language used depended very much on the aim of particular lessons. For example, a lesson designed to introduce a new topic contained many questions on that topic in English if the main content area was background, or in German if the main stimulus was a text on that topic. Other lessons, particularly those which were mainly grammatical in content, or where examination techniques were being practised, tended to be conducted mostly in English. The tables which follow have been calculated as follows: for each content area observed during the recorded lessons, percentages are given, for either German (target language) or English (mother tongue). This percentage represents the proportion of times the particular content area was carried out in either language. In addition, a third category, 'Both', is coded separately, representing decoding, where the teacher says something in German followed by the translation into English. To give an example: if a teacher has been recorded on six occasions distributing homework using German three times, English twice and both languages on one occasion, this would be presented as follows:

Content area	Target language	Mother tongue	Both
Homework	50	33.3	16.7

It is the percentage of time devoted to each language which is measured, as opposed to the number of instances a content area was covered.

It was not possible to compare exactly the content of the lessons with the teachers' self-report forms, since the lessons did not contain each content area mentioned on the self-report form and, not surprisingly, there were aspects in lessons which were not mentioned on the forms.

The Tables numbered 3.3.1 to 3.3.5 list the core content areas in the same order as those listed on Table 1.1 which presented the content areas as rated by the teachers themselves. Other areas which were contained in the lessons of individual teachers appear at the end of each table. There was found to be an overlap in certain topic areas, such as 'Correcting' which refers to correcting of any kind, for example of pronunciation, grammar or written exercises. This usually depended on the nature of the correction. For example, correcting of a written exercise done in German involved use of the target language, whereas English answers were usually corrected in English. Pronunciation and grammar were usually corrected through German. Where a further explanation of the grammatical rule was stated, this was coded as 'Grammar'. Grammar itself may appear from the tables below to have higher values in German than indicated by teachers on the self-report sheets. This can be explained by the fact that many of the incidental explanations were given in German, such as examples followed by a brief explanation of the rule, whereas there were very few grammar lessons as such.

In order to give some idea of comparison, details of the following teachers are presented in the tables which follow: the two teachers who emerged consistently as high target language users (T3 and T7), one in the middle category (T4) and the two who ranked as low target language users (T6 and T8). Graphs of the profiles of all the teachers, according to the video evidence, are contained in Appendix F.

HIGH TARGET LANGUAGE USERS

The following two tables (Table 3.3.1 and 3.3.2) show the proportional breakdown by content area for the two teachers who scored highest in their use of the target language both in the self-rating sheet and on the pupil evaluation.

High target language user — Teacher 3

Table 3.3.1   Content areas observed: Teacher 3

Content area	Target language	Mother tongue	Both
Greeting/Settling	100	–	
Introducing	100	–	–
Instructions	100	–	–
Moving on	100	–	–
Vocabulary	66.7	33.3	
Tests	–	–	–
Grammar	100	–	–
Examination techniques	–	–	–
Praising	100	–	–
Correcting	100	–	–
Background	–	–	–
Discipline	–	–	–
Summarising	100	–	–
Questions (text)	100	–	–
Questions (general)	100	–	–
Questions (personalised)	100	–	–
Homework	100	–	–
Incidental	100	–	–
Humour	100	–	–
Checking compr.	100		

The lessons taught by T3 were conducted almost exclusively in German, as evidenced by Table 3.3.1. They consisted largely of questions and answers on listening texts, or revolved around a grammar area such as adjective endings or dative pronouns. The lessons involved several personalised questions directed at individual pupils in order to focus on the grammar point, followed by a very brief explanation, oral practice in the form of pairwork, written practice with follow-up questions and exercises either from the textbook or on the OHP. Table 3.3.1 shows that the only area where any English was used at all was in 'Vocabulary' and the 33.3% represents three out of only nine instances where a quick translation of a word or phrase was given to verify the meaning. For example: T: '*Kleiner* is shorter of distance or size'. There were no other instances of mixing languages or inconsistent use of the target language.

Several areas in the observed lessons have much higher percentages for the target language than those indicated on the T3's self-report sheet which can be partly explained by the fact that some of the areas were not observed during the recorded lessons, such as 'Tests', 'Examination techniques', 'Background' and

'Discipline', all of which were reported as being done at least 25% of the time in English. Moreover, the other areas where the teacher coded English as being used at least some of the time, were viewed in the recorded lessons as conducted in German, for example 'Grammar' and 'Correcting'. T3's lessons contained a fairly large number of instances of incidental language and humour which made the lessons enjoyable and interesting for the pupils and provided them with several instances of extra input, examples of which will be analysed in a later section.

High target language user — Teacher 7

Table 3.3.2   Content areas observed: Teacher 7

Content area	Target language	Mother tongue	Both
Greeting/Settling	100	–	–
Introducing	100	–	–
Instructions	100	–	–
Moving on	100	–	–
Vocabulary	94.8	–	5.3
Tests	100	–	–
Grammar	72.2	27.8	–
Examination techniques	–	–	–
Praising	100	–	–
Correcting	100	–	–
Background	–	–	–
Discipline	–	–	–
Summarising	–	–	–
Questions (text)	100	–	–
Questions (general)	100	–	–
Questions (personalised)	100	–	–
Homework	100	–	–
Incidental	100	–	–
Humour	100	–	–
Checking compr.	100	–	–

The teaching style of T7, the second highes target language user, was similar in many ways to that of T3. Extensive use was made of the OHP. The grammatical constructions which were to feature in the lesson first emerged from initial warm-up or lead-in questions. These were then discussed and practised in context, usually consolidated by pairwork and written exercises with follow-up. The quantity of German used by this teacher was also similar to that used by T3, with only 'Grammar' and to a lesser extent 'Vocabulary' involving any English at all. Furthermore, comparison with the self-report sheet completed by this teacher reveals that the video-recordings represent higher use of the target language than estimated by him. It will be recalled, however, that this teacher admitted during the interview session that the video-recordings represented an increase in German from his normal classroom practice. This shows, as was the case with T3 above, that although this teacher was identified as one of the highest users of the target language on the basis of the self-report sheet, the evidence recorded on video indicates an even higher level of target language use. Although this represents a greater percentage of target language than normal, however, there was absolutely no evidence at all throughout the video-taped lessons to suggest that the pupils were uncomfortable with this. It does reveal, though, that 100% use of German most of the time was perceived by this teacher as indicative of good practice.

The target language provided by T7 had many qualities which will be identified at a later stage. It contained several incidental phrases, humour, relatively advanced constructions and was most of the time comprehensible to most of the pupils. The quality of the German was highlighted by a native-speaker as being particularly effective and authentic.

Average target language user — T4

Table 3.3.3   Content areas observed: Teacher 4

Content area	Target language	Mother tongue	Both
Greeting/Settling	100	–	–
Introducing	75	–	25
Instructions	65.5	13.8	20.7
Moving on	87.5	–	12.5
Vocabulary	49.1	14.5	36.3
Tests	–	–	–
Grammar	50	33.3	16.7
Examination techniques	–	100	–
Praising	62.5	25	12.5
Correcting	100	–	–
Background	100	–	–
Discipline	100	–	–
Summarising	–	–	–
Questions (text)	19.6	70.6	9.8
Questions (general)	89.2	4.6	6.2
Questions (personalised)	96.0	–	4.0
Homework	60.0	–	40.0
Incidental	94.1	5.9	–
Humour	85.7	14.3	–
Checking compr.	100	–	–

The lessons of T4, the selected average target language user, consisted of mainly the revision of a topic or the introduction of a new topic. Much was teacher directed and consisted of questions on the topic or personalised introduction to a topic. The areas of 'Greeting/Settling', 'Correcting', 'Background', 'Discipline' and 'Checking for comprehension' were conducted entirely in the target language, although most of them represented very few occurrences (Greeting/Settling 2; Comprehension checks 2; Discipline 1). Similarly, the 'Examination techniques' recorded as 100% English was a single occurrence. The most significant element of this teacher's performance was the regular use of a mixture of the target language and mother tongue. The following examples illustrate the general pattern of this teacher's use of the languages which permeated many of the lessons:

T4

T:[. . .] that's right, one single shop, es
gibt nur einen einzigen Laden. Es ist ein   [there is only one single shop.
kleines Lebensmittelgeschäft.   It is a small grocer's shop]
What do you learn about this shop?

T: OK. Schlagt schnell die Bücher auf   [OK. Open your books quickly
Seite 60. OK, would you check your spellings   at page 60 . . . Now we're going
please with the ones in the box in the book.   to speak a little. No, first of all
OK. Jetzt sprechen wir ein bißchen. Nee,   we'll do a listening exercise.]
machen wir zunächst Hörverständnis. Take a
look at the table here in Nr. 1. Was sucht er oder sie?

The constant switching between languages within sentences, which was a feature of all the content areas, makes this teacher's use of German difficult to follow. This type of code-mixing differs from decoding in that the utterances are not translated from the target language into the mother tongue, but parts of the sentences are in one language and parts in the other. The teacher herself commented that this had been pointed out to her by a language inspector, although she was convinced that this was the particular style with which she was comfortable.

The self-report of T4 indicated five areas where 100% target language was said to be used ('Instructions', 'Moving On', 'Praising', 'Correcting' and 'Personal Language'), only one of which is confirmed by the classroom observation ('Correcting'). A small percentage (4%) of 'Personalised questioning' was conducted in both languages, but the majority of personalised questions (96%) was conducted entirely in German. 'Grammar', 'Vocabulary' and 'Examination techniques' were noted by this teacher as being done more in English, which is confirmed by the video-recordings in one case ('Examination techniques') with 'Grammar' and 'Vocabulary' containing significant proportions of English and German mixed. The pupils also noted a significant proportion of language mixing in four out of the six areas (see Appendix E), with English featuring largely in 'Grammar' and to a lesser extent in 'Background', 'Homework' and 'Discipline'. The only area where the class was 100% sure that German was used was 'Class language', which could be interpreted as containing 'Instructions', 'Moving on', 'Correcting', 'Praising' or 'Checking for comprehension', some of which are confirmed in the observed lessons.

LOW TARGET LANGUAGE USERS

Profiles of the two teachers who ranked as the lowest on the target language score on their own self-report sheets (T6 and T8) appear below.

Low target language user — Teacher 6

Table 3.3.4   Content areas observed: Teacher 6

Content area	Target language	Mother tongue	Both
Greeting/Settling	–	100	–
Introducing	–	–	–
Instructions	16.1	67.7	16.1
Moving on	25	75	–
Vocabulary	21.6	74.4	4.0
Tests	–	–	–
Grammar	–	100	–
Examination techniques	–	–	–
Praising	50.0	46.0	4.0
Correcting	22.2	66.7	11.1
Background	–	–	–
Discipline	–	–	–
Summarising	–	–	–
Questions (text)	59.6	38.2	2.2
Questions (general)	40.0	60.0	–
Questions (personalised)	–	–	–
Homework	–	100	–
Incidental	33.3	58.3	8.3
Humour	–	100	–
Checking compr.	–	100	–

This teacher followed a set routine which remained absolutely constant throughout the recording period and which, therefore, one might assume to be fairly representative of usual classroom practice. Each lesson began with the page number spoken in German, followed by the English equivalent. The text was read aloud by the teacher, interspersed with pupil repetition, followed by a translation given by the pupils, which the teacher then repeated or corrected. Unfamiliar words were repeated in chorus and written on the blackboard.

Comprehension checks in English were frequent, to ensure that every word and every phrase had been understood. Grammatical constructions were then explained in English and practised using the exercises in the textbook.

The profile of T6's lessons is heavily weighted towards English with only two areas with target language values of 50% or above ('Praising' and 'Questions on a text'). Decoding was infrequent with only 16.1% as the highest value for 'Instructions', representing 5 out of 31 instances. English was by far the predominant language and was used consistently for 'Greeting/Settling', 'Grammar', 'Homework', 'Humour' and 'Checking for comprehension'. This bears a very close similarity both to the teacher's own view of her practice and to the views of the pupils.

Low target language user — Teacher 8

Table 3.3.5   Content areas observed: Teacher 8

Content area	Target language	Mother tongue	Both
Greeting/Settling	100	–	–
Introducing	50.0	50.0	–
Instructions	81.8	18.2	–
Moving on	100	–	–
Vocabulary	42.1	18.4	39.5
Tests	–	100	–
Grammar	14.3	82.8	2.8
Examination techniques	–	100	–
Praising	93.8	6.2	–
Correcting	80.0	20.0	–
Background	85.7	14.3	–
Discipline	–	100	–
Summarising	100	–	–
Questions (text)	100	–	–
Questions (general)	–	–	–
Questions (personalised)	100	–	–
Homework	20	80	–
Incidental	66.7	33.3	–
Humour	75.0	25.0	–
Checking compr.	100	–	–

T8 was teaching a fifth form class which was preparing for GCSE examinations and, therefore, many of the recorded lessons focused on examination practice and techniques for performing well in the exams. Some lessons began with a warm-up session, usually linked to oral practice for the examination, others concentrated on written aspects with some grammatical explanations and practice. There was a general insistence on accuracy as opposed to communication throughout the lessons, even in the initial warm-up, which was probably indicative of practice for an examination.

T8's use of the target language reveals a consistency of use between German and English, with only 'Vocabulary' involving any significant amount of decoding. Six areas were noted where 100% target language is used, ('Greeting/Settling', 'Moving on', 'Summarising', 'Questions on text', 'Personalised questions' and 'Checking for comprehension'), representing general classroom language and questions on a text, which are generally done by most teachers in the foreign language. Only three areas were done completely in English ('Tests', 'Examination techniques' and 'Discipline'), with 'Grammar' relatively close at 82.8%. Other areas where English was used minimally are 'Instructions', 'Praising', 'Correcting' and 'Background'. There were very few instances of decoding, namely in 'Grammar' with 2.8% and 'Vocabulary' with 39.5%.

Comparison with the teacher's own self-report responses suggests that the videos represent more German than in this teacher's normal classroom practice, although he insisted that this was very much normal practice and apologised for the amount of English he had to use, especially in teaching grammar and explaining examination techniques. In the self-report sheet, five areas were listed as consistently done in English ('Tests', 'Grammar', 'Examination techniques', 'Discipline' and 'Background'). Three of these were confirmed in practice, 'Grammar' was also close, with only 'Background' significantly different from what was recorded on video. One must note, however, that the area of 'Background' was not covered in a specific lesson or lessons, but rather took the form of comments and statements made throughout various lessons. It may be, therefore, that straightforward background lessons would involve more English. There was also a fairly high correlation between the two measures of 'Introducing objectives', and possibly 'Vocabulary' and 'Instructions', if one recalls that the self-report sheets did not allow a coding of 'Both' languages.

The pupil responses revealed similarities with the teacher's own measures on 'Grammar', 'Homework', 'Discipline', and 'Class language'. If one relates the category 'Class language' for pupils to the areas of 'Instructions', 'Moving on', 'Correcting', 'Praising' and 'Checking for comprehension' on the teacher's self-report sheet, this would suggest a balance between languages used. The pupils did not agree as a group that any content area was conducted entirely in German. This would suggest that the elements noted by the teacher and those coded by the pupils represent features of normal practice, but perhaps the general picture conveyed on video is one that more target language was in evidence in the observed lessons than might normally be the case. One must recall that this fifth year class was preparing for the final GCSE examinations, and that significant proportions of the lessons were conducted in German which confirms the finding in the other fifth year classes of T1 and T5 that the approach of the examinations does not necessarily result in a reversion to English.

Examples of content areas

In order to give some idea as to what was meant by the various content areas, the following sections contain examples from various teachers.

GREETING/SETTLING

The language used for this content area consisted of short utterances, and there were very few instances of the warm-up routine which is more common in Key Stage 3.

Habt ihr gerade Lunch gehabt?	[Have you just had lunch?
Habt ihr Mittagspause gehabt? (T1)	Have you just had lunch break?]
Gut . . . also . . . ssh . . . Seid ihr fertig? (T2)	[OK. Are you ready?]
Also. Schnell bitte, meine lieben Leute.	[Right. Hurry up people.
Beeilt euch. Schnell. Schnell. (T10)	Quick. Quick]

INTRODUCING OBJECTIVES

In most cases the introduction of the lesson followed on naturally from Greeting/Settling:

Schauen wir mal, was wir, was wir schon kennen. (T2)	[Let's see what we know already.]
Wir machen heute weiter mit Beschreibungen. Zuerst wollen wir etwas zuhören. (T3)	[Today we're going on with descriptions. First of all we're going to do a listening exercise.]
Alle Bücher weg. Wir brauchen nichts. Wir wollen zuerst ein Video ansehen. (T9)	[Put all your books away. We don't need anything. First of all we're going to watch a video.]

In no lessons was there any comprehension checking of the objectives of the class; if pupils had any difficulty understanding, they had to wait until the activity or the topic started. It was good to see the lessons getting off to a target language start, however.

INSTRUCTIONS

Throughout the lessons instructions were given, either for setting up or concluding activities. In many instances it was difficult to distinguish between utterances which were giving instructions and those which involved moving on to another activity.

Ihr müsst den Text zusammenstellen. (T1)	[You have to build up the text.]
Ich möchte sehen, ob ihr eure Hausaufgaben gelernt habt. Ihr habt fünf Minuten, um zehn Sätze zu schreiben. (T4)	[I want to see if you have learned your homework. You have five minutes to write ten sentences.]
Und ich möchte wissen, wo die verschiedenen Leute hier wohnen. So, erst mal den Namen schreiben bitte und dann diese Fragen beantworten. (T7)	[I want to know where the various people live. So first write your name on the sheet and answer these questions.]

MOVING ON

Many of the phrases used to move from one activity to another are indicated by one word utterances, such as *Also, Jetzt,* and they are usually followed by a pause which indicates that the lesson is about to change activity and/or pace.

Wir haben jetzt noch zehn Minuten. (T1)	[We 've still got ten minutes left.]
OK. Jetzt etwas Anderes. (T3)	[OK. Now for something different.]
OK. Könnten wir das lassen? (T3)	[Right can we leave that?]
Ich glaube, wir machen ein bißchen weiter dann. (T5)	[I think we can move on a bit further.]

The frequency of the internationally recognised OK would possibly help pupils to realise that something was happening, even if they did not understand the rest.

VOCABULARY

Teaching of vocabulary or explaining the meaning of new words featured in most teachers' lessons and in most cases teachers attempted to explain without recourse to English. In the beginners' lessons taught by T2 the vocabulary was taught by flashcards in a variety of ways. In the more advanced lessons, pupils encountered words which were unfamiliar but in many instances they were able to guess the meaning from the general context.

[bunt] Viele Farben draufstehen, das ist bunt. (T3)	[Lots of colours are on it, that's coloured.]
[Noten] Noten in der Schule. A, B, C das sind die Noten. (T4)	[Marks in school. A, B, C are marks.]
[schick] Das ist fast dasselbe Wort. Schick, ja? (T9)	[It 's almost the same word.]

Some teachers avoided delays by simply inserting the correct English equivalent after the explanation or by sandwiching it between the German version.

[Art] Kunst, richtig. Kunst for art, kennen wir. Aller Art means of all sorts. (T4)

[modisch] Ja, things that are fashionable, ja, was modisch ist, ja? (T9)

[selber] eh . . . den gleichen, same. Gut. (T7)

TESTS AND EXAMINATION TECHNIQUES

'Tests' and 'Examination techniques' were dealt with by very few teachers and the examples of the phrases used have been cited above.

PRAISING

Again this was one of the functions which could easily be carried out by one or two word utterances. All of the teachers were observed to praise their pupils, although in most cases it was hard to distinguish the true praise from a simple discourse marker. Most teachers had their set phrases which were used in all lessons:

Ja. Sehr gut. (T1)	[Yes. Very good.]
Das war Spitze. (T2)	[That was great.]
Genau. (T7)	[Exactly.]
Ausgezeichnet. (T9)	[Excellent.]

BACKGROUND

The category of 'Background' was used where teachers referred to aspects of the target country, albeit briefly during lessons.

Und das heißt . . . auf Deutsch gibt es ein Wort für jemanden, der nicht zahlt, und das heißt Schwarzfahren. (T2)

[That means . . . In German there is a word for someone who doesn't pay the fare. The term is fare dodger.]

Man kann hier nicht sitzenbleiben. Aber das kann man in Deutschland machen. Wenn man sehr schlechte Noten bekommt, muß man sitzenbleiben . . . In derselben Klasse. (T8)

[Here you can 't repeat a year. But you can in Germany. If you get bad marks, you have to repeat . . . to stay in the same class.]

In deutschen Häusern hat man sehr oft einen Keller. (T10)

[German houses very often have a cellar.]

All of the information given on the German-speaking countries was very relevant, integrated into the lessons and appeared to be understood by the pupils.

SUMMARISING

There were very few examples of summarising, either to recap what had been done within the lesson or in previous lessons. The main category of summarising was where the teachers repeated pupil utterances for clarification or to summarise various points for the rest of the class.

QUESTIONS

Questioning fell into one of three categories: questions on a text, personalised questions and general questions. Very many of the teachers' utterances were questions, so that it is unnecessary to pick out individual examples. Examples of more lengthy pieces of lessons can be found elsewhere (Neil, 1995).

HOMEWORK

Some lessons began by checking homework, others finished with the homework being distributed to the class. At times the German instructions were supported by the written word on the blackboard, by visual support from the textbook or it was explained again in English.

Hausaufgabe für das nächste Mal . . . für nächste Woche. Dialog üben — Im Fundbüro. Und nächste Woche gehe ich hier mit Mikrophon herum ja um aufzunehmen. Also, fleißig üben. (T7)

[Homework for next time . . . for next week. Practise a dialogue: 'in the lost property office'. Next week I will be going round with the microphone to record your dialogues, so practise them thoroughly.]

Schreibt das bitte ins Klassenheft. Für Morgen. (T8)

Write that into your jotter for tomorrow.]

Und dann werde ich die Hausaufgaben für Montag aufschreiben, ja, die Hausaufgaben für Montag. Morgen sehen wir uns nicht. Also, zuerst lest mal bitte . . . [long explanation]. Is that clear now? You're quite sure you know what you have to do? (T1)

[And then I 'll write up your homework for Monday. Tomorrow I don 't see you. So, first read . . .]

CHECKING FOR COMPREHENSION

This is a very important area and it was used by all teachers as a gauge of how comprehensible the German was and to test whether intervention on their part was necessary to render the input comprehensible. It was evident in all the lessons that the pupils were familiar with the individual teacher's phrases used to check comprehension. Usually pupils responded in the affirmative when asked if they had understood something or if everything was clear. Where something was unclear, the teacher was met with blank stares which acted as a cue for some explanation or assistance.

Habt ihr verstanden? (T1)	[Have you understood?]
Versteht ihr, was ich meine? (T2, T9)	[Do you understand what I mean/ what I'm saying?]
Habt ihr das gehört? (T3)	[Did you hear that?]
Was heißt das auf Englisch? (T8)	[What does that mean in English?]

A danger of such phrases is that pupils simply say 'yes', although they have neither understood what they are supposed to, nor understand the phrase used to check for comprehension. All of the teachers were very experienced, however, and followed their utterance with some strategy for ascertaining whether the pupils had understood or not; for example, they asked for an explanation, or for an interpretation in English, or they got a pupil to demonstrate.

SUMMARY

This chapter has analysed in some detail the quantity of the target language used and the content areas for which it was used. It is necessary, however, to look in greater depth at the quality of the language used.

Chapter 4

Features of the target language

The previous chapter analysed the teachers' presentation of various areas of content recorded during several lessons and compared these findings with the teachers' self-report and their pupils' perceptions. Most of the content areas listed above could be clearly categorised and the labels suggest what the actual content of the language used within these areas might be. This chapter first illustrates in some detail the language content of some of the more loosely defined areas such as 'Incidental Language', 'Humour' and 'Discipline'. These were chosen for further analysis because they go beyond the language related to the objectives of the lesson or the syllabus-speak mentioned by Mitchell (1986, 1988) and Franklin (1990) and are linked to the provision of rich, relevant and comprehensible input. Examples from each category will provide a sample of the German used by those teachers who were able to offer something in addition to the language contained in the coursebook or in other resource materials. The chapter then goes on to describe some of the strategies involved in teaching grammar, correcting and encouraging communicative competence.

Incidental language

The category 'Incidental language' was coded where the teachers' utterances could not fit easily into a set content area such as 'Grammar' or 'Questions on a text'. Examples of 'Incidental language' are additional comments following an answer or explanation or utterances totally unrelated to the immediate task but prompted by an interruption, such as *'Wir haben viele Besucher heute'* (T7) when the class had been interrupted three times by visitors. In some lessons such utterances added to the quality of the language used and gave certain lessons an air of authenticity, although it must be said that in other lessons some incidental language simply caused bewilderment in pupils and did not enhance the quality of the learning. The effect of such incidental use of language can be measured by pupils' reactions and responses, which are in many instances very clear from the video recordings, although they do not emerge in the transcripts. The incidental language can be categorised under various headings.

THE 'HERE AND NOW'

Most examples adhered to the 'here and now', that is to say that they related to the present situation in class, so that the pupils had contextual clues to support the utterances of the teacher. They either referred to the work being done by commenting on an answer, providing further information, or giving the teacher's opinion on a subject. Even if pupils were unable to understand the exact meaning of these phrases and although in most cases they would have been unable to use the same phrases themselves, the extra utterances created a more authentic target language environment. Examples of some of these 'here and now ' phrases are as follows:

Es war ein bißchen zu schnell. (T3)   [It (=the speed of the tape) was too fast.]

Es war viel zu leicht. (T4)   [That was far too easy.]

Zu schwierig ist das. (T9)   [That is too difficult.]

All of the above examples consist of simple phrases. Teachers tended to have a set repertoire of such phrases which they used throughout the lessons, such as those referring to the level of difficulty of a certain exercise or those acting as redundant phrases in order to allow more time, either for the pupils to think or for the teacher to organise equipment.

ADDED COMMENTS

Another type of incidental language contained supplementary information to a question or answer provided by the pupils:

Ja, oben, unten. Oben, unten. Das war   [Yes, upstairs, downstairs.
eine Fernsehsendung, ja? Kennt ihr die   That was a TV programme,
Sendung? (T10)   wasn't it? Do you know the programme?]

Nein, ich hatte keine Schokolade.   [comment during role play guessing game]
Ich nehme ab. (T9)   [No I didn't have any chocolate. I'm slimming]

[Es wird bald regnen]. Das ist für   [It will rain soon. That's perhaps
Nordirland, vielleicht. (T5)   the case in Northern Ireland.]

Other examples related to the teachers' own opinion on a topic or were comments on pupils' answers. Again these phrases were incidental and not essential to the lesson but they added to the flow of target language to which the classes were exposed:

Also das ist Geschmacksache.(T10)   [Well, it's a matter of taste.]

Nein, ich glaube nicht. (T8)   [No, I don't believe so.]

Ich denke, es geht.(T4)   [I think that's acceptable.]

No attempt was made by the teachers to check whether the pupils had understood these phrases and, indeed, no understanding was necessary. The most important aspect of such phrases is that they provided pupils with undiluted target language which was designed to atune their ears and create an environment where English was minimised. Clearly these phrases would not have gained any response had they been in English.

THE FOREIGN LANGUAGE ASSISTANT (FLA)

One of the ways in which teachers have been able to increase the amount of target language used and the authenticity of the language produced in class is by involving the foreign language assistant in lessons. Some teachers prefer to give small groups to the assistant, whilst others involve them in team-teaching situations. The study by Franklin (1990) showed that involving other teachers in lessons can be beneficial in raising the level of target language.

T1 employed Hans, the German assistant, as a tape-recorder, as a dictionary, as a provider of background information and as a means of creating an environment where a need for genuine communication could be created. It gave the teacher the opportunity to demonstrate to the pupils that, when learning a foreign language, learners will have difficulty and will not know all the vocabulary or constructions. This should enhance pupils' confidence to try to speak without fear of making mistakes. The following examples provide illustrations of the FLA serving as a linguistic, background and communicative resource.

1 Linguistic resource

The distinction between '*ich arbeite halbtags*' and '*ich bin halbtags beschäftigt*' is explained:

T1

T: Teilzeitbeschäftigung, OK, ich habe eine	[Part-time job. OK. I have
Teilzeitbeschäftigung or ich arbeite . . .	a part-time job or I work . . .
FLA: [. . .] halbtags.	. . . part-time.
T: Two ways to say the same thing. Ich arbeite	I work part-time.
halbtags.	I think that is the most
FLA: Ich glaube, das ist das, das Verbreiteste.	prevalent expression.
T: Ja eben, so wollte ich gerade sagen.	Yes, I was just going to say that.]

The discussion between teacher and FLA involves so much repetition that the pupils are given extra input. A further example of the FLA as a linguistic resource involves a spontaneous role play situation in order to explain the meaning of the German word '*Kunde*'.

T1

T: *Nein . . . nein. Es ist vielleicht schwer.* [No . . . no. It's perhaps a bit difficult.
Kannst du (to FLA) das auf Deutsch Can you explain that in German and
erklären, und dadurch erkläre ich das auf I'll explain it in English. For example,
Englisch. Wenn ich z.B. in einem if I work in a shop and . . .
Geschäft arbeite und . . .
FLA: *Ich bin . . . ja ich komme 'rein.* I am . . . I come in. I would like
Ich möchte etwas kaufen. to buy something.
T: *Ja, was möchten Sie? Ja, also, was* Yes, what would you like.
möchten Sie? Well, what would you like?
FLA: *Ich möchte eine neue Lampe.* I'd like a new lamp.
T: *Ja, bitte. Hier haben wir mehrere Lampen . . .* Fine. We have several lamps here.
Das ist mein Kunde. That is my customer.]
P: *Customer?*

The high level of understanding and cooperation necessary for such spontaneous situations to arise naturally during the lesson involves good coordination between teacher and assistant.

2 Background and communicative resource

The FLA is used to confirm information about Germany.

T1

T: *Gibt es Mädchengymnasien in Deutschland.* [(to class): Are there all girls' schools
Wißt ihr? in Germany. Do you know?
P: *Ja.* Yes.
T: *Ja? Gibt es? (to FLA). Stimmt das?* Yes (to FLA) Yes? Are there? Is that right?
FLA: *Ich glaube nicht.* No, I don't think so.]

A genuine purpose for communication is created by the teacher at the beginning of a lesson by encouraging the pupils to convey real information to the assistant. Since the assistant is not familiar with many aspects of school life, it gives the topic of school, which would otherwise be difficult to discuss in a genuinely communicative way, a realistic focus:

T1

T: *Hans wird euch eine . . . er hat einige* [Hans is going to ask you
Fragen zu stellen, und zwar über die Schule some questions about school
in England oder Nordirland. in England or Northern Ireland.]

This information gap is maintained throughout this lesson and several instances of genuine communication are evident in discussing school and likes/dislikes.

T1

T: *Habt ihr [diese Schule] gern? Ja? Das* [Do you like this school? Yes?
freut mich. Ja, und warum? I'm glad about that. Yes, and why?
FLA: *Warum?* Why?
T: *Ja. Hans würde gerne wissen, warum?* Yes, Hans would like to know why.]

By emphasising that it is the assistant who wants to know their opinions, the teacher provides an added incentive for the pupils to communicate. Furthermore, situations in the school with which the teacher would be familiar, but where the foreign language assistant has no background knowledge, became communicative for the benefit of the assistant. The well-established practice of collecting money for charity one day in the year by allowing pupils not to wear school-uniform on payment of a sum of money is discussed at length.

Humour

Humour was to be found in most teachers' lessons. Real communication within lessons was evident where humour was introduced, since it revealed that pupils were able to get beyond the form of the utterance and comprehend the intended meaning. The level of comprehension could be judged by their reaction. While it is highly likely that the reaction of the pupils varied according to their level of comprehension, it is also possible that on some occasions they understood but did not find the utterance amusing. The willingness to be humorous in the foreign language also revealed that the teachers had to be confident that their pupils would understand and that the rapport between them would be strengthened rather than weakened by the humour. It is not possible to identify certain humorous strategies, since humour depends on the personality of the teacher and on the relationship between teacher and pupil. In order to illustrate the various types of humour, however, some examples will be cited from several teachers' lessons.

T1

FLA: Habt ihr alle den gleichen Studenplan oder habt ihr unterschiedliche?	[Do you all have the same timetable or different ones?
Ps: Ja.	Yes.
T: Jeder. Ja, wir haben keine Antwort gehört . . . Also Hans hat gefragt, habt ihr alle denselben oder verschiedene. Da habt ihr alle 'ja' gesagt (pupil laughter). Aber er hat euch eine Wahl gegeben.	Each. Yes, we didn't hear an answer. Hans asked you if you have the same or different ones. And you all said 'yes', but he gave you a choice.]

The above is an example of the teacher resolving incomprehension with humour and providing comprehensible target language in so far as the pupils can understand from the context that something is not correct and are able to respond appropriately following the teacher's interventions.

Explaining ideas is also done in a humorous way with little recourse to English and even involving pupils in attempting to be humorous:

T1

[explaining one of the arguments for
keeping school uniform]

T: *Ja, stellt euch mal vor, Karen ist sehr
reich und Kathrin ist sehr sehr arm. Und
wenn es keine Uniform gäbe, ja, dann würde
Karen sich . . . was für Kleider würde
Karen anziehen?*

P: *Besser Kleidung.*

T: *Bessere Kleidung . . . und was für
Kleidung würde Kathrin anziehen?*

P: *Keine.*

T: *Mm. Das wäre interessant. Ja. Sie würde
nur Fetzen, rags, sie würde nur Fetzen
anziehen können, ja, also sie würde . . . was
für Kleidung würde sie . . . sie würde sich
trotzdem Kleidung anziehen müssen, sie
könnte nicht nackt herumlaufen. Sie würde
bessere Kleidung tragen, und Kathrin würde . . .*

[Imagine that Karen is very rich and
Kathrin poor. If there weren't any
uniform, what kind of clothes
would Kathrin wear?

Better clothes.

Better clothes . . . and what
sort of clothes would Kathrin wear?

None.

Hm. that would be interesting,
wouldn't it? She would only be
able to wear rags. Yes, well,
she would have to wear some kind
of clothes, she couldn't
run around naked.]

This is an interesting example since it is far more complex from a grammatical point of view than the previous examples, but achieves its aim because of the context of the imaginary situation and because of the key vocabulary. Pupils respond to the scenario, however, despite the fact that they are probably unfamiliar with the conditional tense, and they are certainly not familiar with the conditional with modals and the imperfect subjunctive used as the conditional. It is therefore an instance of a contextually clear example despite the linguistic complexities.

Humour was used in an integrated way by this teacher (T1) and it provided pupils with opportunities to react and respond to utterances with little, if any, output. The pupils were comfortable with the teaching style and appeared to be at ease with the varied input provided.

Correction by humour was a feature of T4's lessons:

T4

T: *Louise, was tut weh?*

P: *Meine Magen tut weh.*

T: *Meine Magen? Wieviele Magen hast du
denn? Hundert? Wenn du meine Magen
sagst, dann hast du zwei, drei oder vier.
Was solltest du sagen?*

P: *Mein Magen.*

[Louise, what hurts?
I have a sore stomachs (plural ending)
My stomachs. How many stomachs
do you have? If you say 'meine'
then you have two, three or four.
What should you say?
Mein.]

Another teacher used humour in commenting on a pupil's answer:

T7
[role play scenario led by the teacher
following the pattern: What have you lost?
Where?]

T: *Wo hast du dein Messer verloren,*
Andrew?
P: *Ich habe ihn im Schwimmbad verloren.*
T: *Im Schwimmbad. Das Messer, nicht?*
Das Messer. Wo hast du dein Messer
verloren?
P: *Ich habe es in dem Schwimmbad . . .*
T: *Er hat das Messer im Schwimmbad verloren.*
Da müssen wir es finden . . . aber schnell, nicht?

[Where did you lose your knife,
Andrew?
I lost it (wrong gender) in the
swimming baths.
In the swimming baths. Knife is neuter.
Where did you lose your knife?
I lost it in the swimming baths.
He lost the knife in the
swimming baths.
Then we better find it and quick!]

The supplementary comment made following the pupil's answer momentarily detracts from the grammatical accuracy insisted on in the exercise and focuses pupils' attention on the meaning rather than on the grammatical construction.

The humour provided by T7 is related to the pupils' knowledge of the world and their own personal experience, although not to the 'here and now' of the classroom. While it is very simple in linguistic terms, it added an extra dimension to the rapport which existed between teacher and pupils which was commented on by the panel of judges and by the transcriber. The pupils' spontaneous reaction to the humorous remarks suggested that they were at ease in the target language.

Some attempts at humour were, unfortunately, lost on the pupils of T10, partly because they did not appear to understand the joke, or because they were unfamiliar with the vocabulary. In asking questions about articles of clothing, the teacher tried to make a humorous remark at the expense of the only male pupil in the class:

T10
T: *Was für eine Strumpfhose trägst du,*
Robert?

[What kind of tights are you wearing,
Robert?]

Perhaps Robert understood more than it appeared; he had given up German before this project had finished. On the topic of house, on the other hand, when the teacher is trying to get the pupils to say which rooms they had in their homes, the pupils found the exaggeration amusing:

T10

T: *Was sind sie für Zimmer?*	[What rooms are they?
P: *Fünf Schlafzimmer.*	Five bedrooms.
T: *Unten? Im Erdgeschoß? Aha. Also, diese*	Downstairs? On the ground floor?
Familie schläft nur (laughs at own joke).	So this family only sleeps. They don't
Sie essen nicht, sie waschen sich nicht, . . .	eat, they don't wash, they don't
sie sehen nicht fern, sie machen nichts, eh,	watch TV, they do nothing,
nur schlafen sie, ja? (pupils laugh). Ihr habt	only sleep. Do you only have
nur Schlafzimmer im Hause, oder?	bedrooms in the house?]

SUMMARY ON HUMOUR

The presence of humour in the classroom may be an indicator of good practice and of good provision of the target language. It also provides some indication as to the pupils' comprehension of the German used by the teacher. Moreover, it is evidence that using the target language is not necessarily damaging to the rapport between teacher and pupils. The observations suggest that the teachers who used humour and whose humour was responded to appropriately by the pupils were more confident in their use of German and that their pupils were more used to hearing it as the normal language of communication.

Discipline

The function of disciplining in the target language is one where many teachers said they would be more inclined to use English. On the self-report sheet the mean score was 1.4 (where one teacher indicated 75% English and 25% German). During the recordings, most classes were so well behaved that it was not necessary to discipline at all. Only two teachers had cause to use the target language to intervene in any disciplinarian way, T4 (one instance) and T10 (fifteen instances). Some examples where these teachers did use the target language to carry out this function are cited below in order to demonstrate the language used.

T4's one example relates to a pupil not having learned vocabulary:

T4

T: *Denkt ihr . . . Andrew hat seine Vokabeln*	[Do you think Andrew learned
nicht gelernt? Ich denke, er kann besser lesen,	his vocabulary? I think he can
als lernen. Das nächste Mal bitte besser lernen.	read better than he can learn.
	Next time learn them better please.]

T10's class was the one which required most intervention of the ten classes videoed, partly because of their low ability and partly because they came from a variety of previous teachers. Various phrases are used by this teacher to discipline the class in German:

T10

T: *Louise, kannst du das? Kein Buch mitgebracht? Na ja, typisch. Haben wir ein Buch für zwei Personen? Das ist unverschämt. Unverschämt. Also, ich glaube das nächste Mal bekommt ihr eine Strafe? Ja. OK? Das nächste Mal müßt ihr das Buch mitbringen.*

[Louise, can you do it? You haven't brought your book with you? That's typical. Do we have a book for two. That's a disgrace. A disgrace. Well the next time, you will get a punishment exercise. The next time you must bring your book with you.]

The problem of not having a book is regarded as serious in this class and the teacher repeats the *unverschämt*, although it is unclear whether or not the pupils understood the word. They were aware, however, that the teacher was displeased with them by her tone of voice, if not by the content of the utterances. Despite the fact that they may not understand, T10 resists the temptation to decode in order to convey her annoyance to the pupils.

On another occasion, a minor intervention was simply *Was ist los?* when pupils were talking as the teacher was explaining something. Exasperation was expressed when a pupil was not at the correct page:

T: *Das ist aber nicht zu glauben. Seite 46 ist das.*   [It's unbelievable. Page 46.]

One technique used by this teacher to discipline is referring to the time they went to bed the previous evening as an explanation for their inattention in class. One such example is given:

T10

T: *Lisa. Das geht nicht. Meine Güte. Also, Lisa, um wieviel Uhr bist du gestern abend ins Bett gegangen? Lisa. Lisa. Wann bist du gestern abend ins Bett gegangen, Lisa?*
P: *Um 11 Uhr.*
T: *Um 11 Uhr. Zu spät! Geh heute morgen, heute abend früher ins Bett, bitte. Sonst mußt du immer so in meiner Klasse gähnen. Das ist so deprimierend.*

[Lisa. That 's not on. For goodness sake. Well, Lisa, what time did you get to bed last night?
At 11.
At 11. Too late. Go to bed this morning, this evening earlier. Otherwise you'll be sitting yawning in my class. It's so depressing.]

Unfortunately this does not seem to have been an effective remedy, since the pupil seemed to remain inattentive. On other occasions, short phrases are used to deal with situations:

T: *Lisa. Jetzt hört's auf!*   [Lisa. Stop that now!]

T: *Ich verliere langsam Geduld!*   [I 'm gradually losing patience!]

T: *Strafe, ja!*   [Right, punishment exercise!]

T10 had indicated on the self-report sheet that she used German 75% of the time in disciplining and the 66.7% calculated on the observation is very close to this. The examples cited above reveal that in most cases the syntax is very simple, with simple verbs and tenses. Despite this, it would be difficult to ascertain whether or not the pupils had understood the content except by the threatening tone of voice. However, as such the input provided by the teacher may be regarded as comprehensible.

Teaching of grammar

The previous parts of this chapter have detailed the language used by teachers to cover various aspects of lessons. Johnstone (1995) has argued that it is not sufficient simply to provide the pupils with a rich diet of the target language. He states that it is necessary to include the explicit teaching of grammar, which he calls Explicit Positive Evidence (EPE), and also that it is necessary to provide some correction of errors, which he terms Explicit Negative Evidence (ENE). With a language such as German, the grammatical structure of which becomes difficult quite early on, it is necessary to integrate the teaching of grammar with the communicative aspects of the language at the outset. It is also necessary to correct errors in order to avoid compounding difficulties in comprehension.

The following sections look at the ways in which the project teachers introduced and developed the grammar of German, how they led their pupils to master the new constructions and how they corrected erroneous utterances.

As an introduction it must be said that all teachers consciously taught the structure or form of the language to some degree, depending on the focus of particular lessons. For most classes, which had reached Book 2 of *Deutsch Heute* (Sidwell and Capoore, 1991), the main grammatical features to be dealt with were comparative adjectives, adjective endings and the imperfect tense; other classes were focusing on different aspects of the language. As might be expected, however, it was not always the new grammatical items which caused problems. In order to impose some order on the various strategies used by teachers, these will be categorised under the grammatical headings: nouns, pronouns, adjectives, verbs, prepositions and word order, although the strategies used to teach one element of grammar may well be the same used to teach others.

NOUNS

Gender is generally considered to be an important aspect of learning German, since the fact that there are three possibilities makes it more difficult than French. The fact that only few examples follow suggests that, by this level, pupils are familiar with the concepts of gender and case, and that the main focus of attention must be to incorporate new vocabulary into their existing gender schema. Aids such as the colour coding introduced by T9 were useful to help pupils remember. T2 particularly, whose pupils had begun German relatively recently, concentrated on genders of newly encountered vocabulary, and the class of T5 was revising for the GCSE, so that fine-tuning of genders was an issue. In the first example below T2 points out that the gender is incorrect and raises her voice in anticipation of hearing the correct one. In the second example T5 gives the pupil a choice between two definite articles:

T 2

P: der Jugendherberge.
T: Nicht der, sondern . . .?

[the youth hostel.
not *der*, but . . .]

T5

T: der oder das?

Metalanguage in the target language to describe the genders is introduced by T9 and it is obvious that the pupils understood the terms used, integrating the new words into the colour scheme:

T9

T: Also, Jeans, ja das ist weiblich, mit rot geschrieben, und Kuli, das ist männlich, mit blau geschrieben.

[Well, jeans is a feminine word, written in red and pen is masculine, written in blue.]

T: Ja, paß mal auf. Also, Bluse ist weiblich. Ja? Also man sagt eine Bluse.

[Be careful. Blouse is feminine. OK? Therefore, you say *eine Bluse*.]

T: Also, bitte paß mal auf! Der Regenschirm. Also beschreib den Regenschirm.

[Please be careful here. *Der* umbrella, so describe *den* umbrella.]

Metalanguage in German is also used as a summary point by T7 prior to pupils' working in pairs:

T7

T: 'Wir haben' und 'es gibt' mit Akkusativ: Wir haben ein Sofa. Es gibt ein Bücherregal. Aber hier mit 'der' aufpassen! Wir haben einen Teppich.

[The phrases 'we have' and 'there is' take the accusative case. We have a sofa. There is a book-case. But here with masculine nouns be careful. We have *einen* carpet.]

T10 also ensures that gender metalanguage was known in an example which involved gender and prepositions:

T10

T: Aber hier ist das Dativ. Steht auf der Zufahrt, das ist Dativ hier. Ja? Auf? Aber das ist die Zufahrt. Weiblich ist das.

[Here it is in the dative case. It is sitting in the drive-way, that is dative here because of the *auf*. But it is *die* drive-way. It's feminine.]

T: Das ist männlich. Der Garten, Akkusativ also den Garten.

[It's masculine. *Der* garden. Accusative, therefore, *den*.]

These examples are interesting, because T10 is the only one who was consistent in teaching the main grammatical sections through English and who stated in the interview that she did so. It appears from these examples, however, that despite this, the pupils had no problems with the metalinguistic terms used.

PRONOUNS

German pronouns are extremely difficult to teach since they look fairly similar but have different meanings depending on the context. Pupils find it difficult to differentiate especially between pronouns such as *ihm/ihn/ihr/ihnen/Ihnen*. The video-recordings provide examples of the teaching of the dative and accusative forms of pronouns by Teachers 1, 3 and 7. The techniques used by all three teachers attempting to teach these points were similar. First they demonstrated the structure by using several examples, they then encouraged pupils to respond to isolated questions, sometimes by providing scaffolding, which helped to build up their answers. Only when they had developed some initial confidence in using the structure were pupils given a pre-communicative or communicative task and the lessons concluded with a grammar note which was copied from the OHP.

T1, for example, teaches the dative pronouns by personalising the topic. Firstly, she collects items from the pupils in the class and then proceeds to ask whom they belong to:

T1

T: Gehört dir das?	[Does that belong to you?
P: Nein.	No.
T: Gehört dir das, Jane?	Does that belong to you, Jane?
P: Nein.	No.
T: Gehört dir das, Fiona?	Does that belong to you, Fiona?
P: Ja.	Yes.
T: Ja, das gehört mir.	Yes, that belongs to me.
P: Ja, das gehört mir.	Yes that belongs to me.]

This allows the pupils to hear the question several times before they have to respond, and the answer is finally fed to the first pupil by the teacher. This technique is continued until the pupils are thoroughly familiar with the structure which the teacher then changes to the third person :

T: Gehört ihr das?	[Does that belong to her?]

This very communicative way of introducing the dative pronouns by personalising the structure seemed to be effective with this class and they were confident in its use before the end of the lesson.

T3 also introduced the dative pronouns, especially with the impersonal verbs *passen* (to fit, go with), *gefallen* (to like) and *stehen* (to suit), all in the context of personal appearance. Once again this was done in the following example by illustration, made as communicative as possible by referring to the 'here and now' and by personalising the topic, taking examples from the class:

T3

T: Ich habe kurze Haare, und ich glaube, ich meine, kurze Haare stehen mir gut. Also, lange Haare würden mir nicht gut stehen, finde ich (one pupil laughs), ja? Wie ist es mit Louise. Hat sie kurze oder lange Haare?	[I have short hair and I think that short hair suits me. Long hair wouldn't suit me, I think. What about Louise. Does she have short or long hair?
P: Lange Haare	Long hair.
T: Lange Haare. Und wie stehen ihr lange Haare? Wie stehen ihr lange Haare? Stehen ihr lange Haare gut oder . . .?	Long hair. And how does long hair suit her? Does it suit her or . . .
P: Gut.	Well.]

Much of the work was done by the teacher on this topic with pupils providing one word answers, and indeed in the first lesson on the topic they were not asked to use the structure at all. A later lesson on clothes based on an OHP transparency develops the grammatical features highlighted in the previous lesson, but this time the pupils are led gradually to the point where they have to use the structure:

T3

T: Wie ist es mit ihm. Paßt die Hose ihm, gut oder nicht?	[What about him? Do the trousers suit him or not?
P: Er paßt.	They (wrong pronoun).
T: Die Hose. Sie . . .	It's *die* trousers. They . . .
P: Sie paßt.	They suit.
T: paßt . . .	suit.
P: ihm nicht.	don't suit.
T: Sie paßt ihm nicht. Warum paßt sie ihm nicht?	They don't suit him. Why do they not suit him?
P: Sie ist zu kurz.	They're too short.]

In this example the teacher immediately follows the correct grammatical structure provided by the pupil with a question related to the meaning, which indicates that there is a focus on communication, facilitated and supported by the newly practised dative pronoun. The exercise is concluded with a paired activity where pupils are asked to put the various constructions together:

T3

P1: Gefällt dir mein Rock?	[Do you like my skirt?
P2: Nein, sie steht dir nicht.	No, it doesn't suit you.
P1: Warum nicht?	Why not?
P2: Er ist dir zu eng.	It's too small for you.]

At the end of this series of lessons these pupils appeared to be competent in the use of the nominative, dative and accusative pronouns with all genders.

As stated above, the focus on the communicative aspect of the grammar makes the exercise meaningful for the pupils who are encouraged to use it within a context, as opposed to learning the rules *per se*.

T7 also taught pronouns, especially the use of nominative and accusative, again embedded in a topic context, namely lost property, and he focused on several aspects of the language simultaneously. He very skilfully introduces the accusative pronoun by first allowing pupils to gain confidence using the perfect tense of *verlieren* with the accusative noun and the following preposition. This involves quite a considerable amount of constructing on the part of the pupils. When confidence is gained, the teacher makes a substitution for one of the pupils and proceeds with various examples of the feminine pronoun followed by the masculine pronoun in the accusative:

T7

T: *Wo hast du deinen Koffer verloren, Nicholas?*	[Where did you lose your suitcase, Nicholas?
P: *Ich habe . . . er . . . im Café verloren.*	I lost it (wrong grammatical case) in the café.
T: *im Café verloren. OK. Ich habe . . .*	Lost in the café. OK. I lost..
P: *Sie.*	It (wrong gender)
T: *Nein, der Koffer.*	No, *der* (m) suitcase.
P: *Er.*	It (wrong case)
P: *Ihn.*	It (correct case)
T: *Ihn. Gut. Ich habe ihn . . . wo verloren?*	It. Good. I lost it . . . where?]

It is clear that the use of the accusative prepositions was not new, but the putting the whole sentence together was. The support provided by T7 helps to focus attention on the isolated words, whilst not losing sight of the communicative aspect, since he continues to press for the answer *wo verloren?* The same pattern is adopted for the neuter pronoun. Interestingly the teacher does not concentrate on the feminine and neuter which remain the same in the nominative and accusative, before introducing the masculine accusative, since it might have caused transfer problems.

The examples cited above illustrate the similarity in the teaching styles of T3 and T7; they both introduce a grammatical item into the lesson, firstly by demonstration, then by inserting examples into controlled exercises, providing support, gradually allowing pupils more freedom to use the language and culminating in a semi-structured, pre-communicative paired-activity. It is also worth noting that the classes of both T3 and T7 were within one chapter of the textbook, having begun learning German at the same time. Of course these grammatical points would have to be revised again several times in order to permit pupils to be creative in their use of the structures.

ADJECTIVES

The two main aspects of adjectives which were taught in the corpus of lessons analysed were adjective endings and comparatives, both of which appear in the second book of *Deutsch Heute*. Adjective endings are parts of German grammar with which foreign learners continue to have great difficulty since the endings and the various rules simply have to be learned. Apart from the set phrases taught in the textbook, such as *das alte Rathaus, die alte Brücke*, pupils find it very difficult to use adjective endings spontaneously.

Many teachers felt the need, in addition to correcting wrong endings used by pupils, to raise their awareness of when an ending was necessary and when not by questioning them and contrasting two forms of the adjective:

T1

T: Warum gibt es nette, steht drin, nette,	[Why does the text say *nette*, etc
zuverlässige, aber man sagt doch, man sagt,	and yet you say she
sie soll nett und zuverlässig sein. Warum?	should be *nett*? Why?]

This question from the teacher elicits the response that the noun is feminine. The teacher then points out the position of the adjective and states, in English, that the adjective takes an ending when it appears before the noun.

Similarly, T9 uses metalanguage and questions pupils on the difference between predicative adjectives and adjectives requiring an ending:

T9

T: Wann brauchen wir eine Endung? Also,	[When do we need an ending?
wir können mal sagen, das Rathaus ist	We can say the town hall is historic,
historisch, der Damm der Riesen ist	the Giant's Causeway is world-famous
weltberühmt, also wir brauchen keine	so that we don't need an ending
Endung. Versteht ihr, was ich meine? Wann	in this case. Do you understand
brauchen wir eine Endung?	what I mean?
P: When the adjective comes before the noun.	When do we need an ending
T: OK. Wenn das Adjectiv vor dem Wort	on the adjective?]
kommt. When the adjective comes	
before the noun.	

The pupil's response in English shows that he has not only understood the metalinguistic question but is also familiar with the rule. The teacher's use of decoding here is designed to confirm the pupil's response and this leads on to a quick revision of the various endings and finally the adjective tables being copied from the OHP in English.

Other teachers simply had to remind pupils of the correct form of the adjective by providing the stem of the word and pausing to allow pupils to insert the correct ending:

T5

T: im vorig . . ? Was kommt am Ende?	[last . . . What comes at the end?
P: s?	-s?
T: Nein, mit Dativ.	No in the dative case.
P: n?	-n?
T: vorigen Jahr, ja.	*vorigen* year, yes.]

A raising of consciousness in the pupil resulted in some guess work, although in the end she got it correct.

Comparative adjectives are dealt with by one teacher. Examples are taken from several different topic areas, comparing people, mountains and cars. Pupils are then in a position to supply the correct form of the comparative:

T3

T: Wie ist diese Frau?	[What's this woman like?
P: Schlanker.	Slimmer.
T: Sie ist schlanker. Sie ist schlanker	She's slimmer. She's slimmer
als die erste.	than the first one.]

This pattern continues, whereby the teacher provides support to enable the pupils to insert the correct form of the comparative adjective. When she is confident that pupils have mastered the form, she transfers it to more communicative questions and personalises the grammatical point to ask about brothers and sisters and which ones are older or younger. This transfers the focus of the lesson from the pre-communicative to the more communicative domain where pupils can see the value of what they have learned in order to enhance topics which they already know. Following this, a written explanation is given and is copied by the pupils from the OHP.

This approach which gave pupils the opportunity to use the forms first in a tightly structured way, leading to more freedom and culminating in an exploration and explanation was indicative of the teaching style of the high target language users.

VERBS

There was no formal teaching of a new tense in the lessons recorded, with the exception of the grammar taught by T10 through English. These lessons were designed to summarise all the pupils knew about verbs up to that point. Other classes were acquainted with the present, the perfect and the imperfect tense, and some teachers used German metalanguage to remind pupils of these:

T5

T: Die meisten Verben sind im Imperfekt.	[Most verbs are in the imperfect.
Sie was..? Das war im Imperfekt. Sie machten?	They were doing,
OK? Sie machten, ich machte, sie machten.	I was doing, they were doing . . .]

At another time the teacher elicits the correct imperfect form of the verb:

T5

T: Was ist das Imperfekt von sein?	[What's the imperfect tense
Ich bin, ich . . ?	of 'to be'?
P: War.	War.]

The conditional is taught by T1 in the topic of future plans and occupations:

T1

T: Ich würde. Ja? Ich würde gern. Wiederholt. Ich würde.	[I would. Yes? I would
Ps: Ich würde.	like to. Repeat. I would.]

Because of its similarity to its English equivalent and to the German form of the future with which pupils were already familiar, the teacher simply demonstrates with this one example and asks pupils to repeat.

PREPOSITIONS

A further difficulty in German grammar for foreign learners is posed by prepositions, especially ones which can take more than one case. In beginners' lessons the main focus was on the basic prepositions which take the dative within the topic of directions. This lesson is fairly standard for practising the prepositions and directions according to *Deutsch Heute 1,* Chapter 5. This beginners' class would have done this some time ago, however, so that the lesson must have been revision in preparation for development into the next topic. Use of the prepositions by the pupils in this example would be unconscious since they would have learned the set phrases *an der Ampel, auf der linken Seite,* but would as yet be unfamiliar with the grammatical rules.

T7 endeavoured to teach the difference in case use with prepositions which could take either the accusative or the dative. In addition to the complex use of prepositions he used the three verbs *stecken, legen* and *stellen* which can cause problems of their own. In the following examples this teacher uses scaffolding to provide stepping stones for the pupils, although one gets the impression that the stepping stones do not provide help so much as answer the questions for them. The teacher begins the lesson by using realia in the classroom to demonstrate the different verbs to put. He puts the book into the cupboard and then takes it out, moving to the table where he places it face down and then he places it upright, giving a running commentary as he does so:

T7

T: Also, ich stecke das Buch nicht in den Schrank, und ich lege das Buch nicht auf den Tisch. Ich stelle das Buch auf den Tisch. Also, wenn etwas aufrecht ist, so eine Lampe oder so, man stellt das auf den Tisch. Wenn ich es so mache, lege ich es auf den Tisch. Und wenn ich etwas in den Schrank tue, dann stecke ich das in den Schrank. Paßt auf!	[So, I'm not putting the book into the cupboard, I'm not putting the book onto the desk. I am putting it (upright) on the desk. So, when something is standing, like a lamp or something like this, the verb is *stelle* it on the desk. If I put it like that the verb is *lege* and if I put it into the cupboard the verb is *stecke.* Be careful!]

This explanation is followed by several examples in which the teacher elicits the correct case by providing scaffolding:

T7

T: Ich lege das Buch auf . . ?	[I put the book on . . ?
P: Tisch.	Table.
T: Auf . . ?	On . . ?
P: Den Tisch.	The table.
T: Ich lege das Buch auf den Tisch. Gut.	I put the book on the table. Good.

Den Tisch. Akkusativ. Wo ist das Buch?	The table. Accusative. Where is the book?
P2: Das Buch ist . . .	The book is . . .
T: Das Buch ist auf . . .	The book is on . . .
P2: Dem Tisch.	The table.
T: Auf dem Tisch. Dativ.	On the table. Dative.]

It is evident from this example that the pupils are not confident about using the structure, so the teacher then reverses the roles and, in order to enable the pupils to hear several more examples, he gets them to ask him the question: *Was machst du mit dem Buch?* He then gives several more examples and finally provides the rule for the prepositions in English.

WORD ORDER

Word order is extremely difficult for learners of German since the rules are different from English. Examples were found in the lessons of two teachers (T4 and T8) where word order in subordinate clauses was highlighted. T4 begins by using the construction as it first appeared in *Deutsch Heute 1* in the context of 'travel and weather':

T4

T: Wie kommst du zur Schule, wenn das	[How do you get to school, when
Wetter schön ist? Ich schreibe die erste Hälfte.	it's nice weather. When . . .
(writes on b/b) wenn . . . das . . . Wetter . . .	the . . . weather . . .
schön . . . ist.	is . . . nice.]

This is followed by pupils' providing several examples of the same structure, using the written form as support. The structure is then transferred to the context of family. Following several examples in this context, where the topic becomes personalised (e.g. 'How do you feel when your brother is bad?' 'How do you react when your parents are angry?'), the teacher then moves to the structure using *'weil'* (because). This development is essential with this grammatical topic, since many pupils tend to fossilise at the stage of the context in which subordination is first met. Changing the subordinate conjunction and altering topic are, therefore, vital to helping pupils work independently with subordinate clauses.

During an orally based lesson, the *wenn*-clause structure is revised and pupils are encouraged to use the construction actively, sometimes with great difficulty.

T8

T: *Und Paul, was ziehst du an, wenn du ins Bett gehst?*	[Paul, what do you put on when you go to bed?
P: *Wenn ich in Bett gehst.*	When I go (wrong ending on verb) to bed.
T: *Bitte?*	Sorry?
P: *Wenn ich ins Bett gehst . . .*	(repeats)
T: *Gehe . . . Aha.*	*gehe*
P: *Eh. zehe ich*	I put (wrong verb)
T: *Zi.zi.zi*	Zi, Zi
P2: *(to the first pupil) Just say trage.*	Just say 'wear'.
P: *Trage ich . . .*	I wear . . .
T: *Nein . . . ziehe ich . . .*	No, I put on . . .
P: *Ziehe ich mein Shorts an.*	I put on shorts.]

Such practice, although communicative, in the sense that there is an information gap, is designed to practise the structure and lexis. The fact that the second pupil realises that the same communicative function could be fulfilled by a different, more straightforward verb, both from the point of view of pronunciation and word order, suggests that the class views the exercise more as one of communication than of grammar practice. It is also worth noting that, despite the fact that the structure appeared first in the teacher's input and was used several times in examples by him, the pupils still have difficulty in producing the longer utterances, since they have to concentrate on the word order of verbs, the agreement of the verbs, the correct positioning of the separable prefix, the correct gender and case of the articles of clothing. Therefore, although they are able to understand the target language used, their ability to produce the structure is much more limited.

SUMMARY ON TEACHING GRAMMAR

The paragraphs above illustrate various techniques employed by teachers to raise pupils' awareness of the main points of German grammar through the target language, namely highlighting items; using metalinguistic terms (especially those similar to their English equivalents); personalising grammatical forms; demonstrating and illustrating; questioning; contrasting; scaffolding; providing a communicative framework and explaining the rule. It is perhaps noteworthy that most examples quoted are from teachers T1, T3, T7 and T9 who rank as the higher target language users in the group.

Error correction

'Error correction' in this section refers to instances of teachers' correcting erroneous or ambiguous utterances. Language teaching has moved on from thinking that pupils simply imbibe the correct structures if they hear them used, as many of the examples above have illustrated. Unlike the youngster learning his or her native language, the language teacher in the classroom, as was argued earlier, has to cope with several limitations. Error correcting can refer, however, to more than just the correcting of erroneous grammatical utterances. Van Lier (1988) mentions three areas which may require correction, namely errors of fact, of reasoning and of language. The transcripts provide evidence of some error correction mainly of language and of fact, although there are fewer instances than one might expect from a classroom language learning situation.

LANGUAGE ERRORS (1) — PRONUNCIATION

In all the transcripts there were few examples where the teacher had to correct the pupils' pronunciation. This is possibly because they had been learning German for at least two years, and the fact that German pronunciation is fairly straightforward. The main problems were the vowel sounds *a/e; ei/ie; au/ü* and the dipthong *äu*. The most direct way of dealing with errors of pronunciation was simply to repeat the correct pronunciation after the pupils, sometimes, although not always, encouraging them to repeat it after the teacher. In some instances it is not clear whether what the teachers correct are actually errors of pronunciation or points of grammar.

LANGUAGE ERRORS (2) — GRAMMATICAL

Where the errors are grammatical, other strategies are used by the teachers to repair them. In some instances the teachers simply provide the correct grammatical form for the pupils. With more difficult aspects, such as adjective endings, teachers sometimes provide the correct form, or sometimes they repeat the stem of the adjective and allow the pupils to add the correct ending:

T3

T: *Was trägt sie?*	[What's she wearing?
P: *Ein rot.*	A red (no ending).
T: *Ein rotes.*	A red (provides ending).
P: *Ein.*	A.
T: *Ein rotes Haarband.*	A red hairband.]

In other examples, teachers highlight the problem area or provide the necessary basic information, such as the correct gender of the word, which enables the pupils to work with the new information and to incorporate this into their answers. In the following example the correct gender is given, but the pupil is expected to formulate the correct sentence herself:

T3

T: Gefällt dir mein Trainingsanzug?	[Do you like my training suit?
P: Nein, sie steht dir nicht. Es ist . . .	No it doesn't suit you. It's too small.
es ist zu klein.	
T: Nein, Nein. Moment. Gefällt dir mein	No, wait a minute. Do you like
Trainingsanzug. Das ist der Anzug.	my training suit. Suit is masculine.
P: Nein, er steht dir nicht. Er ist zu klein.	No it doesn't suit you. It's too small.]

In this example the pupil is unsure of the gender and thus uses two different ones in order to hedge her bets; when corrected, she is able to construct both sentences correctly.

Another strategy used by teachers was to seek clarification by asking for repetition, either genuinely not having heard or pretending not to have heard in order to encourage the pupils to repeat and possibly self-correct.

Verbs caused difficulties for many pupils, especially in classes where there was an emphasis on form in preparation for forthcoming oral examinations. The main areas of difficulty were in the past participles and auxiliaries used in the perfect tense. The main technique employed by teachers to cope with these recurring errors was to use scaffolding in order to provide support without giving the correct form, since it was generally assumed that pupils knew the underlying rules.

Some pupils were seen to elicit help by pausing or by providing an inaccurate but comprehensible message to the teacher in order that he or she would provide the correct word or grammatical form:

T3

P: Sie hat 130 Mark für ihren . . ?	[She paid DM 130 for her . . ?
T: Ihren.	Her.
P: Ihren Pulli bezahlt.	For her pullover.]

This appears to represent a first step to pupil independence in coping with the language in that the pupil is willing to be creative even though she is uncertain about the structure.

Other teachers tried to encourage the pupils to use the target language to express their answers or to extend their utterances:

T1

T: Ja, kannst du das auf Deutsch sagen?	[Can you say that in German?]

Although it might appear rather artificial and beyond the needs of communication to encourage pupils to extend their utterances, it must be borne in mind that these pupils were practising for the GCSE examination which, although communicatively based, still requires a relatively high degree of accuracy for success at the higher level.

FACT

The correcting of facts is an interesting area because it represents a shift from the traditional function of the target language used by teachers. There were a few examples in the transcripts where teachers, more concerned with the truth of an utterance than the correct grammatical form, sought clarification from pupils. This suggests that in the fourth and fifth forms, lessons are becoming more communicatively oriented.

T8

P: *Die Mittagspause dauert 45 Minuten.*　　　[The lunchbreak is 45 minutes.
T: *Nein, glaube ich nicht. Mehr als 45 Minuten.*　No, I don 't think so. More than
P: *50 Minuten.*　　　　　　　　　　　　　　　45 minutes.
T: *50 Minuten. OK.*　　　　　　　　　　　　50 minutes.]

Some teachers encouraged pupils to seek clarification themselves and well-learned phrases were in evidence in one class in particular, for example the simple statement that the pupil did not know the answer or had forgotten it:

T7

T: *Was ist das?*　　　　　　　　　　　　　　　[What's that?
P: *Ich weiß nicht.*　　　　　　　　　　　　　　　I don't know.
T: *Du weißt nicht. John?*　　　　　　　　　You don 't know. John?
P2: *Das ist eine Tische.*　　　　It's a table (wrong gender ending).
T: *Ein Tisch.*　　　　　　　　　　　　　　　A table.]

T7

T: *Und was hat sie gesagt?*　　　　　　　　　[What did she say?
P: *Vergessen.*　　　　　　　　　　　　　　　Forgotten.
T: *Vergessen? OK. Fragen.*　　　　　Forgotten? OK. Ask
P: *Was hat du gesagt?*　　　　What did you say (wrong ending)?
P2: *Letztes Jahr war ich in Frankreich*　　Last year I was in France
und habe Paris besichtigt.　　　　　　and I visited Paris.
P: *Letztes Jahr hat sie . . .. [to other pupil]*　　Last year she was . . .
Was hast du . . ?　　　　　　　　　　What did you . . ?
P2: *Letztes Jahr war ich in Frankreich*　　Last year I was in France
und habe Paris besichtigt.　　　　　　and I visited Paris.
P: *Letztes Jahr war sie in Frankreich*　　Last year she was in France
und hat Paris besichtigt.　　　　　　and she visited Paris.]

This last example illustrates one of the main objectives in foreign language teaching, namely to get the pupils to use the language meaningfully in context. This pupil (m) genuinely has to communicate with the other pupil (f) and he forgets her utterance twice, but the teacher gives him the time to repeat his question and eventually he gets the answer correct. It is noticeable that the teacher does not correct the grammatical mistakes in the verbs nor does he complete the question for the pupil.

SUMMARY ON ERROR CORRECTION

This section has described a number of strategies used by the project teachers to deal with error correction, such as repetition, pausing, questioning, scaffolding, eliciting the rules and encouraging pupil independence. It is evident that all of the teachers regard this provision of negative input and feedback as part of training the pupils communicatively. The strategies highlighted reveal that many of the teachers do not abandon communication in favour of grammatical accuracy, but rather use the meaning of the utterance to try and push the pupils on to the next stage of accuracy. At times it is a long slow process, as evidenced in some of the examples where multiple errors are committed in one sentence. These sentences, however, contain quite advanced grammatical features and many of them had just been introduced in the textbook. It will take some time, therefore, until pupils are able to use the features independently in their own interlanguage.

Encouraging communicative competence

The main aim of communicative language teaching is to make the pupils communicatively competent; this involves, in addition to the teaching of grammar, sociolinguistic competence, discourse competence and strategic competence. The few instances in the lessons where these aspects were dealt with are listed below.

SOCIOLINGUISTIC COMPETENCE

Sociolinguistic competence is encouraged in occasions where the teacher draws attention to the fact that a certain utterance may be grammatically correct, but inappropriate from a sociolinguistic point of view. From all the transcripts analysed very few examples of a sociolinguistic dimension could be found and most of them contain some element in English:

T1
T: Kann ich Ihnen helfen, this is the polite form, can I help you

T2
T: [was muß ich sagen] Einfach so? He! He   [What should I say. Just like that? Hey
du da, wie komme ich am besten zur Post?   you, how do I get to the post office?]

A similar example is provided by T7 who points to the inappropriate nature of an utterance when addressing the principal of a school:

T7
T: Wenn er dem Direktor sagt: Hi Jimmy,   [If he says to the headmaster; Hey,
sagt er zum Direktor, ja? Das ist sehr frech.   Jimmy. That's very cheeky.]

When explaining the distinction of verb tenses, T10 points to the regional variation in speech:

T10
T: The imperfect, which is different from French. OK? It's the normal tense that you would find used for example in newspaper reports, or if you were reading a German novel. Generally, it would mostly be in the imperfect with maybe sometimes the odd perfect tense mixed in, sometimes in different regions of Germany you would find they would tend to use more the imperfect than another.

In response to a recalcitrant pupil's questioning about why they could not just learn the perfect tense, the teacher gives an exasperated reply:

T10
T: Apart from the fact that we have to learn the language the way they speak it and not the way we want it to be.

From all the transcripts, however, there appears not to be much emphasis on the sociolinguistic element, although it would perhaps be true to say that certain topics would lend themselves more to a sociolinguistic explanation than others.

Communicative competence must involve a balance between the four aspects and as such the lessons here would suggest that this balance still requires to be redressed. There were no examples of strategic or discourse competence in any of the lessons.

NATIVE-SPEAKER ANALYSIS OF LESSONS

In order to gain some insight into how native-speakers of German would react to the lessons taught by non-native-speakers, a group of three student teachers was asked to read the transcripts through. They were asked to comment on the authenticity of the language and on the extent to which the lessons would compare with lessons taught by native-speakers. They were not asked to remark on the standard of the teachers' German, but rather to note down aspects which would highlight the language used as that of a non-native-speaker. Their comments were generally positive.

They commented on the simplicity of the vocabulary and the basic use of verbs and tenses, although they considered these to be acceptable for the classroom situation. One native-speaker raised the issue of the unnecessary and rather artificial use of the future tense, since future ideas are more usually expressed in German by the present tense. The comments relating to structure were generally positive, although it was mentioned that several teachers started sentences and then changed half way through; this applied particularly to teachers who used extended utterances.

Several features which indicated that the utterances were not those of a native German were highlighted, most of which related to the inappropriate use of the redundant words. Those which were mentioned most frequently were: *Vielleicht* (perhaps), *Ja, Also* (well then, therefore), *Das geht* (that's OK), *Eigentlich* (really). In particular, the overuse of *ja* between sentences and *also* was commented on for several teachers. Furthermore the use of *man* (one) in some contexts was inappropriate:

Vocabulary given in the textbook was sometimes mentioned by the native-speakers as inappropriate, for example *die Bude* (booth) as a place to buy tickets; *Jungkoch* (young cook) was changed to *junger Koch*.

Incorrect word order was identifed by the native-speakers in several transcripts. It would appear, however, that they misread the punctuation or the punctuation had been misinterpreted by the transcriber.

These were the main comments made by the native-speakers of German on the lessons taught by the non-native teachers. Over 120 minutes of recording for ten teachers, it is encouraging to note that overall they were fairly convinced by the teachers' use of German and that the idiosyncracies noted either were overuse of fairly redundant words or were explicable in the context.

CONCLUSION

This chapter examined in greater detail, with examples from the transcripts, various aspects of the German provided by the teacher. It was seen that the teachers, especially those identified as high target language users, made extensive use of the target language, but at the same time that they made it accessible to the pupils at an appropriate level. The final chapter brings together a number of strands from various parts of the study.

Chapter 5

Reflections on the target language

The previous chapters have systematically looked at the use of German by the ten project teachers from three standpoints: firstly from the teachers' perspective, secondly, from the pupils' viewpoint and finally from the video-recorded lessons.

Quantity of target language

From all perspectives it was seen that very few teachers used the target language exclusively, and those who did use it 100% of the time had not estimated as high a level in their practice. This confirms the views expressed by the teachers surveyed by Dickson (1996). It is perhaps now becoming clear that the dogmatism of the early days of communicative language teaching has passed and that teachers are now able to teach according to their own convictions. When asked in the questionnaire if they were using German in the classroom at a level which they considered appropriate, all of the teachers responded affirmatively.

The results of this study seem to suggest, however, that teachers' use of the target language has increased in recent years, although direct comparisons with previous studies is not possible because of the different purposes and contexts of these studies. The amount of target language used in general for most of the content areas by most teachers far exceeds the findings of Parkinson et al (1982) who found that the foreign language was restricted to 'greetings'. The quantity of target language used by the teachers in this study also exceeds the findings of US studies. Hedderich (1992), for example, found that teachers spoke 59% of the total lesson time and 29% of that time was in German. Wing's (1980) study of Spanish and the investigation of Duff and Polio (1990) into teachers' use of several languages at higher education level revealed a great variation in teachers' use of the language.

The lack of substantial use of the target language by pupils (see Table 3.2.3) shows, in accordance with the findings of Mitchell (1986), that most of the work done in class was teacher-dominated. Despite most teachers' insistence, during the interviews, on encouraging pupil participation in the lesson and on interaction and opportunities to use the language, in many classes there was a remarkable paucity of such opportunities, relative to the amount of teacher talk. Unlike the findings of Mitchell, however, the data indicate that the tasks pupils were asked to do were not too simple. The probable reasons for the difference is that the pupils in this study were older and that the target language is now much more a feature of lessons than was the case in the days of the Scottish study.

German or English?

It has been established that very few teachers in this study used German 100% of the time, therefore, one must conclude that all of them concurred with Buckby (1985) and Atkinson (1993) that there is a place for the mother tongue in the foreign language classroom. The main question, therefore, relates to the areas where German was used and those which were carried out in English. Most teachers used the target language 100% for the main routine functions such as 'Greeting/Settling', 'Moving on', and 'Praising', and for some teachers German was used 100% of the time in the wider areas of 'Personalised language' and 'Questions on a text'. The areas which were treated in English were mostly 'Grammar' and 'Vocabulary', even by the highest target language users (T1, T3, T7 and T9). These represent the areas which required either specialist knowledge or clarification in English and they are similar to the areas mentioned by the teachers' in the studies of Wing (1980), Mitchell (1988) and Franklin (1990) as requiring some use of the mother tongue. These are also the two areas identified in the most recent UK survey, where the majority of teachers noted that explaining meanings and teaching grammar could be done with difficulty (Dickson, 1996).

All teachers seemed to have a clearer idea about the content areas which were consistently carried out in English than about those which are consistently done through the target language, similar to the finding of Mitchell (1986).

Quality of input

The first question to be asked of the quality of the target language provided by the teachers is whether it was comprehensible. Much of the German was directed at the 'here and now' of the classroom environment, although some lessons dealt with topics which went beyond the bounds of the classroom. In many cases the target language was rendered comprehensible by using extralinguistic and paralinguistic cues, such as demonstrating with visuals, tone of voice and references to contexts which were familiar to the pupils, by use of repetition, substitution, pupil involvement, exemplification and scaffolding many of which are strategies mentioned by pupils in the interviews.

Comprehensible extra target language was a feature of some of the lessons in terms of incidental language and humour which were not part of the lesson objectives but represented spontaneous unscripted speech to which pupils responded. This type of linguistic richness was evidenced not only in the lessons of the most communicative teachers, high target language users (T1, T3, T7 and T9), but also in the medium target language users (T2 and T4) and even in the lessons of the lowest target language users (T8 and T10).

One of the criticisms which could be levelled against the teachers' German here is that it was overall rather simplified and in many lessons it did not seem pitched at an appropriate level for pupils at Key Stage 4. Full details about the grammatical complexity of the teachers' German are found in Neil (1995). The main area of simplification was word order, which remains one of the most difficult aspects of the German language for non-native-speakers to master; complex word order was only evident in the lessons designed to practise such structures. Teachers were seen to use very few subordinate clauses and preferred to use two sentences rather than combine them either by a subordinate or a co-ordinate construction. Another area where simplification was evident was in the tenses of verbs used. Most of the teachers' utterances were based in the 'here and now' and, as a result, dealt in the present tense. With the current emphasis on the visual element in communicative classrooms, however, it is perhaps not suprising that the present tense is used more than any other tense.

Teaching strategies

The examples quoted in the previous chapter illustrate several techniques used by the teachers to teach grammar, in many cases in an integrated communicative way, and examples of strategies used to correct errors were given.

The lessons of all the teachers contained evidence of both implicit and explicit grammar teaching. All the lessons of some teachers contained some grammatical structure which was either being presented or revised. In most cases the lessons were built round a communicative framework, although it was clear to the teacher that the main focus of the lesson was on the presentation and practice of a particular structure. All teachers practised what they preached, therefore, in introducing grammatical elements into their teaching; they all stated in the interview that grammar was essential to the learning of the language within the classroom and all endeavoured to provide it. The approach used, however, was very much communication-oriented and in most lessons items of grammar were presented partly in a target language context with some explanation in English. In some cases it was evident that the pupils were unaware of the focus on grammatical items and were keen to communicate the meaning using other structures. This demonstrates that the teachers in this study did not appear to be under the misapprehensions of communicative language teaching mentioned by Edmunds (1995). In only one set of lessons, that of T10, was there evidence of a traditional approach to new grammar which was introduced by explanation and followed by a written grammar note, all in English. In the course of the video-recordings an inbuilt grammatical progression was evident in the lessons of most teachers, although firmly established within the topic areas as presented in the coursebook. Whilst the syllabus was still topic-based and functional/notional, it was evident that the syllabus followed by most teachers had a clear grammatical spine, such as that mentioned by Brumfit (1980), which underpinned their course.

In the correcting of errors teachers also practised what they preached in that there was consistency between what they said in interview and what they did in practice. All of them corrected errors, but not simply for the sake of grammatical accuracy *per se*. The various strategies used were highlighted in the previous chapter and it was seen that they encouraged communication following correction.

The main criticism of many of the activities in lessons, despite the positive aspects highlighted, must be that they failed to get beyond a pre-communicative stage (Littlewood, 1981), that is to say that the pupils were able to use the structures but they were never required to use them in **genuinely** communicative situations where the focus was not on the grammatical structure. Where paired activities were done, for example, the main items to be used had just been practised; never was there an extended exercise where they had to use a variety of structures acquired over time. In many of the examples quoted, the phenomenon of previous methodologies was evident, where the pupils were confident with the new structures at the time of practice but were unable to integrate these new structures into their overall communicative repertoire.

Indeed, from the evidence one might question whether the approach adopted in these classrooms was really communicative at all. For a more detailed analysis of the extent to which these lessons were communicative, the reader is referred to Neil (1995).

Interpreting the findings

In the introduction, the recent OFSTED report was cited which commented on the lack of use of target language by teachers at Key Stage 4 in comparison with their use of the language with Key Stage 3 pupils. The findings of this study indicate that the pupils of many teachers in grammar schools in Northern Ireland are being given a realistic diet of target language at Key Stage 4 both in terms of quantity and quality. It is significant, however, that even the highest target language users in this study, when reporting on their practice, indicated levels of the target language far below the 100% notional level, but that in the video-recordings they increased their practice. It has been said by one language inspector that the battle of ensuring teacher use of the target language has been won to a large extent. What must remain an area of concern, however, is the lack of pupils' use of the language, an area which may be the focus of future studies.

The last words

In conclusion, the last words go to the teachers who reflected on their practice, who subjected themselves to a year of observation and questioning and who were the main focus of the investigation. They were asked how being involved in this project and in the process of reflecting on the target language had changed their views or their practice

Teacher 3

Despite the regrets during the research project that I had agreed to take part, the fourth form German class warranted concentrated and detailed preparation. However, I would have to admit that taking part in the programme was beneficial from a professional development viewpoint, as I was obliged to re-examine my teaching methods and practices and to make a conscious effort to focus on the target language in the classroom. But it is true to say that this conscious use of the target language had a knock-on effect and benefited other classes too. It is also true that the pupils became more at ease with this increased use of the target language and it was reassuring that the class responses in the questionnaire at the end of the project confirmed this. There is no doubt that in light of the changes which have been made to the GCSE and 'A' level languages syllabuses, target language teaching will of necessity become the norm. There should always be room in the modern languages classroom for flexibility. Too often in the past, new practices have become dogma — to be adhered to at all costs. I feel that the teacher's professional judgement as to how much target language is appropriate, taking into account the ability of the class and the level of difficulty and the nature of the task involved, should always remain paramount.

Teacher 4

The benefit in participating in this project for me was that it forced me to reflect on the most effective way to teach each element of the lessons, i.e. to what extent it would be helpful to use the target language. A secondary benefit was the additional enjoyment for the pupils of being video-recorded — I had an extrovert class!

I did reflect on my usual practice as I was making an effort to use the target language, but in retrospect I feel that I could have explained some points better in English. The script of the lessons was very enlightening. I did not realise how much I 'hopped' from English to German and vice-versa. I could not say that having been involved in the project has influenced my practice greatly. The experience gave me some ideas as to what works well and which things definitely don't. Pressure on time for preparation is one of the main factors which militates against my using more target language.

Teacher 7

I found my involvement with the 'German in the classroom' project to be personally very worthwhile and the article 'German in the classroom: what the pupils think' (Neil, 1996) is now part of our department library. The experience gave me a definite focus for thinking about target language use and was a valuable way of reflecting on lesson planning and the balance between teacher and pupil activity, as well as target language use. Since doing the classes on video I would say that I have continued to use more target language overall and, even when this has lapsed, I have remained more conscious of the issues. Chief among these is the nature of pupils' use of language. Video lessons tended initially to concentrate though on teacher use of language, but it is possibly more important to explore how to motivate and support pupils in target language use. The GCSE results for this class were particularly good. We are currently reviewing our policy on the target language in light of the proposed exam syllabi; the knowledge that this year's exam rubrics would be in the target language concentrated both pupils' and teachers' minds wonderfully. Judicious use of English can be a quicker and more effective way of 'getting at' the target language than a dogmatic avoidance of all use of English.

Teacher 8

I agreed to participate in the research with some trepidation — after all, this was not going to be a simple case of 'observation'; an analysis of every minute of the lessons, with specific parameters, is certainly something which would be guaranteed to put a teacher under pressure and which not every teacher would agree to. My other slight concern was that, children being children, the pupils would 'play up' during the sessions thus creating on tape a false impression of my classroom management skills. As it turned out, however, my fears were unfounded. Both the pupils and I soon forgot that the camera was there — we acted 'normally' which, I feel, is vital in empirical research of this kind. In addition, I made a conscious decision not to alter my teaching style or the content of the lessons simply to put on a good show for the camera. An example illustrates the point: I was aware that the amount of pair- or group-work was being analysed, yet there was very little of this in the sessions taped. Pair-work is a very useful strategy, particularly in junior classes, and I use it a great deal — but only when it is appropriate to the lesson. I use it less in Year 12 where time is at a premium and preparation for the GCSE is paramount. The same goes for use of the target language. The less said about group-work the better! (I note, with a wry smile, that current 'thinking' is once again inclining towards whole-class teaching!)

However, I have no idea whether it was in response to the sessions or to educational reform or some combination, but I have certainly moved to a situation whereby target language is the norm in Forms 1 to 4 and lower VI and almost all lessons in Forms 1–4 involve some pair-work. For Forms 5 and upper VI much grammar work and most exam preparation are still done in English, though this is obviously changing with the new GCSE and 'A' level syllabi.

What I can say with certainty is that participation in the sessions forced me in a way to reflect on my practice. Having perused the findings, I realised that I could use the target language more (comparisons are based on the assumption that all participants acted likewise in not altering their practice for the tape!). Yet I felt satisfied that my practice produced good results and that, as a general rule, practice must be appropriate to the level, ability and ultimately the needs of the pupils. Being under such close scrutiny also prepared me better for the general inspection which took place not long after. Perhaps the conclusions that I can draw from this are that:

- teachers are still learners;

- teachers must move away from the behind closed doors situation and be much more prepared to observe and be observed in aiming to develop as educators (appraisal is, after all, only round the corner!);

- talking about strategies, etc, as for example following the taped sessions, is beneficial to both parties and is essential if ideas are to be shared and development is to take place. This openness is something which I, as Head of Department, encourage in and, indeed, expect of staff.

CONCLUSION

Reflecting on classroom practice, in particular on the target language, has had some benefit on general teaching, according to the teachers who evaluated their experiences. A future activity might be to encourage both teachers and pupils to take another step forward and focus on the amount of pupil use of the foreign language.

The following points should be addressed in any future research exercise:

- how can teachers encourage pupils to use more of the target language in class?

- how can we make our courses more relevant to pupils' perceived communicative needs?

- how can we get pupils to use the language for genuine communication?

In short, how can we move on to what Johnstone (1988) has termed 'second generation' communicative methodology?

References and bibliography

Allwright R, *Observation in the language classroom* (London and New York: Longman, 1988)

Allwright R and K M Bailey, *Focus on the language classroom: an introduction to classroom research for language teachers* (Cambridge: Cambridge University Press, 1991)

Atkinson D, 'The mother tongue in the classroom: a neglected resource?' in *English Language Teaching Journal*, 41, 4: 241–47 (1987)

Atkinson D, 'Teaching in the target language; a problem in the current orthodoxy' in *Language Learning Journal*, 8: 2–5 (1993)

Bahns J, 'Der Input im Fremdsprachenunterricht' in *Bielefelder Beiträge zur Sprachlehrforschung*, 15: 131–45 (1986)

Beeching K, 'Grammar is dead. Long live system-building' in *British Journal of Language Teaching*, 27, 2: 95–98 (1989)

Bleasdale C, *Motivating modern language pupils in S1 and S2*. Paper given at Scottish CILT Conference on Communicative Language Teaching, 11 March 1995, University of Stirling (1995)

Breen M P, 'Authenticity in the language classroom' in *Applied Linguistics* 6, 3: 60–70 (1985)

Brumfit C J, ''Communicative' language teaching: an educational perspective' in Brumfit C J and K Johnson (eds): 183–91 (1979)

Brumfit C J, 'From defining to designing: communicative specifications versus communicative methodology in foreign language teaching' in *Studies in Second Language Acquisition*, 31, 1: 1–9 (1980)

Brumfit C J (ed), *Learning and teaching languages for communication: applied linguistic perspectives* (London: CILT, 1983a)

Brumfit C J, 'Some problems with Krashen's concepts 'acquisition' and 'learning'' in *Nottingham Linguistic Circular*, 12, 2: 95–105 (1983b)

Brumfit C J, 'Must language teaching be communicative?' in Little D, B Ó Meadhra and D Singleton (eds): 11–19 (1986)

Brumfit C J (ed), *The practice of communicative teaching*. English Language Teaching Documents no 124 (Oxford: Pergamon, 1986)

Brumfit C J and K Johnson, *The communicative approach to language teaching* (Oxford: Oxford University Press, 1979)

Buckby M, 'The use of English in the foreign language classroom' in Green P S (ed): 50–67 (1985)

Burstall C, M Jamieson, S Cohen and M Hargreaves, *Primary French in the balance* (Windsor, Berks: NFER, 1974)

Byram M, 'Foreign language education and cultural studies' in *Language Culture and Curriculum*, 1, 1: 15–32 (1988a)

Byram M, ''Post-communicative' language teaching' in *British Journal of Language Teaching*, 26, 1: 3–6 (1988b)

Canale M, 'From communicative competence to communicative language pedagogy' in Richards J C and R W Schmidt (eds): 2–28 (1983)

Canale M and M Swain, 'Theoretical bases of communicative approaches to second language teaching and testing' in *Applied Linguistics*, 1, 1: 1–47 (1980)

Canale M and M Swain, 'Some theories of communicative competence' in Rutherford W and M Sharwood Smith (eds), 61–84 (1988)

Carroll J B, *The teaching of French as a foreign language in eight countries* (New York: Wiley (1975)

Centre for Information on Language Teaching and Research (CILT), What is meant by a 'communicative' approach to modern language teaching? Information Sheet 12 (London: CILT, 1989)

Chambers F, 'Promoting use of the target language in the classroom' in *Language Learning Journal*, 4: 7–31 (1991)

Chambers G, 'Teaching in the target language' in *Language Learning Journal*, 6, 66–7 (1992)

Chaudron C, *Second language classrooms: research on teaching and learning* (Cambridge: Cambridge University Press, 1988)

Clark J L, 'Syllabus design for graded levels of achievement in foreign language learning' in *Modern Languages in Scotland*, 18: 25–39 (1979)

Clark J L, *Curriculum renewal in school foreign language learning* (Oxford: Oxford University Press, 1987a)

Clark J L, 'Classroom assessment in a communicative approach' in *British Journal of Language Teaching*, 25, 1: 9–19 (1987b)

Collins P, 'The moving target' in *Languages Forum*, 1, 1: 16–18 (1993)

Cook V, 'The poverty-of-the-stimulus argument and multicompetence' in *Second Language Research*, 7, 2: 103–117 (1991)

Cook V, *Linguistics and second language acquisition* (Basingstoke: Macmillan, 1993)

Das B K (ed), *Communicative language teaching.* Selected Papers from RELC Seminar, Singapore, 23–27 April 1984 (1985)

Department of Education and Science/Welsh Office (DES/WO), *Modern foreign languages for ages eleven to sixteen* (London: HMSO, 1990)

Department of Education for Northern Ireland (DENI), *Good practice in education. Paper no 2: modern languages teaching in Northern Ireland* (Bangor: DENI, 1985)

Department of Education for Northern Ireland (DENI), *The Northern Ireland curriculum: modern languages. Programme of study and Attainment Targets* (Bangor: DENI, 1992)

Department of Education for Northern Ireland (DENI), *Secondary education 1994: language studies* (Bangor: DENI, 1994)

Dickson P, *Using the target language in modern foreign language classrooms.* Unpublished review paper (Windsor, Berks: NFER, 1993)

Dickson P, *Using the target language: a view from the classroom* (Slough, Berks: NFER, 1996)

Dodson C J, *Language teaching and the bilingual method* (London: Pitman, 1967)

Downes P J, 'Graded examinations for elementary language learners: the Oxfordshire project' in *Modern Languages*, LIX, 3: 153–56 (1978)

Duff P A and C G Polio, 'How much foreign language is there in the foreign language classroom?' in *Modern Language Journal*, 74, 2: 154–66 (1990)

Edmunds M, *Applying research to communicative language teaching.* Paper given at Scottish CILT Conference on Communicative Language Teaching, 11 March, 1995, University of Stirling (1995)

Ellis R, *Understanding second language acquisition* (Oxford: Oxford University Press, 1985)

Ellis R, *Instructed second language acquisition* (Oxford: Basil Blackwell, 1990)

Evans C, 'A cultural view of the discipline of modern languages' in *European Journal of Education,* 25, 3: 273–82 (1990)

Færch C and G Kasper, 'The role of comprehension in second language learning' in *Applied Linguistics,* 7, 3: 257–74 (1986)

Faltis C, 'A Commentary on Krashen's input hypothesis' in *TESOL Quarterly,* 18, 2: 352–9 (1984)

Felix S W and H Wode (eds), *Language development at the crossroads* (Tübingen: Gunter Narr Verlag, 1983)

Flanders N A, *Interaction analysis in the classroom: a manual for observers* (Ann Arbor: University of Michigan, 1960)

Franklin C E M, *The use of the target language in the French language classroom: co-operative teaching as an aid to implementation* (Unpublished PhD, University of Edinburgh, 1990)

Gass S M and C G Madden (eds), *Input in second language acquisition* (Rowley, MA: Newbury House, 1985)

Green P S (ed), *York papers in language teaching* (York: University of York, 1985)

Gregg K R, 'Krashen's Monitor and Occam's razor' in *Applied Linguistics*, 5, 2: 79–100 (1984)

Gregg K R, 'Review of Krashen: the input hypothesis' in *TESOL Quarterly*, 20, 1: 116–22 (1986)

Grittner F M (ed), *Teaching foreign languages,* 2nd edition (New York: Harper & Row, 1977)

Guthrie E M L, 'Six cases in classroom communication; a study of teacher discourse in the FL classroom' in Lantolf J P and A Labarca (eds): 173–94 (1987)

Håkansson G, 'Quantitative studies of teacher talk' in Kasper G (ed): 83–98 (1986)

Halliwell S and B Jones, *On target* (London: CILT, 1991)

Hamilton J, 'Using the target language: from Pilton to Tokyo: a journey through the earth's crust' in *Language Learning Journal*, 10: 16–18 (1994)

Harbord J, 'The use of the mother tongue in the classroom' in *English Language Teaching Journal*, 46, 4: 350–55 (1992)

Harding A, B Page and S Rowell, *Graded objectives in modern languages* (London: CILT, 1980)

Hawkins E, *Modern languages in the curriculum,* revised edition (Cambridge: Cambridge University Press, 1987)

Hedderich N, *Linguistic and communicative aspects of classroom discourse in first year German accelerated learning classes* (Unpublished PhD, Michigan: Ann Arbor University, 1992)

Hermann K, 'What's communicative about asking 'Wo ist die nächste Haltestelle?'' in *British Journal of Language Teaching*, 24, 1: 35–39 (Winter 1986)

Holmes B, *Keeping on target* (London: CILT, 1994)

Holmes J, 'Sociolinguistic competence in the classroom' in Richards J C (ed) (1978)

Hooper J, *Progression in foreign language learning.* Report given at Language World Conference 1–3 April 1995, University of York (1995)

Horner D, 'Acquisition, learning and the monitor: a critical look at Krashen' in *System*, 15, 3: 339–49 (1987)

Hornsey A, 'Authenticity in foreign language learning' in *Languages Forum,* 1, 2/3: 6–7 (1994)

Hyltenstam K, 'Teacher talk in Swedish as a second language classrooms: quantitative aspects and markedness conditions' in Felix S W and H Wode (eds): 173–87 (1983)

Hymes D, 'On communicative competence' in Pride J B and J Holmes (eds): 269–93 (1972)

Johnson K, *Communicative syllabus design and methodology* (Oxford: Pergamon, 1982)

Johnstone R, 'Developing the communicative approach in pre-service teacher education' in Lunt H N (ed): 89–102 (1982)

Johnstone R, *A handbook on communicative methodology in foreign-language learning* (Stirling: Department of Education, University of Stirling, 1987)

Johnstone R, 'Communicative methodology: second generation' in Kingston P J (ed): 12–21 (1988)

Johnstone R, *The role of structure in the development of communicative competence.* Discussion paper for Scottish CILT Conference on Communicative Language Teaching, 11 March 1995, University of Stirling (1995)

Karsten H, 'Probleme des praktizierenden Lehrers mit der Unterrichtssprache' in Voss B (ed): 106–11 (1986)

Kasper G (ed), *Learning, teaching and communication in the FL classroom* (Århus: Århus University Press, 1986)

Kingston P J (ed), *Language breaking barriers*. Selected proceedings from the Joint Council of Language Associations' Annual Conference at University of Warwick, March 1988 (Rugby: JCLA, 1988)

Krashen S D, *Second language acquisition and second language learning* (Oxford: Pergamon, 1981)

Krashen S D, *Principles and practice in second language acquisition* (Oxford: Pergamon, 1982)

Krashen S D, *The natural approach* (Oxford: Pergamon, 1983a)

Krashen S D, 'The din in the head, input and the language acquisition device' in *Foreign Language Annals*, 16, 1: 41–44 (1983b)

Krashen S D, 'Krashen responds to Faltis' in *TESOL Quarterly*, 18, 2: 357–59 (1984)

Krashen S D, *The input hypothesis* (Harlow: Longman, 1985)

Lantolf J P and A Labarca (eds), *Research in second language learning: focus on the classroom*. Delaware Symposium 6 (Norwood, NJ: Ablex Publishing Corporation, 1987)

Little D, B Ó Meadhra and D Singleton (eds), *New approaches in the language classroom: coping with change*. Proceedings of the Second National Modern Languages Convention, Trinity College, Dublin, 31 January and 1 February 1986 (1986)

Littlewood W T, *Communicative language teaching* (Cambridge: Cambridge University Press, 1981)

Littlewood W T, *Foreign and second language learning* (Cambridge: Cambridge University Press, 1984)

Littlewood W T, 'Integrating the new and the old in a communicative approach' in Das B K (ed): 1–13 (1985)

Lunt H N (ed), *Communication skills in modern languages at school and in higher education* (London: CILT, 1982)

Macaro E, 'Target language use in Italy' in *Language Learning Journal*, 11: 52–4 (1995)

McIntyre D, Units for the analysis of teaching behaviour (Unpublished paper, Stirling: Department of Education, University of Stirling, undated)

McLaughlin B, *Theories of second language learning* (London: Edward Arnold, 1987)

Mitchell R, *A review of systematic observation instruments used for the analysis of FL classroom interaction*. Unpublished paper (Stirling: Department of Education, University of Stirling, 1977)

Mitchell R, 'The teacher's use of first language and foreign language as means of communication in the foreign language classroom' in Brumfit C J (ed): 41–58 (1983)

Mitchell R, 'Process research in second language classrooms' in *Language Teaching*, 18, 4: 332–52 (1985a)

Mitchell R, *Communicative Interaction Research Project: final report* (Stirling: Department of Education, University of Stirling, 1985b)

Mitchell R, *An investigation into the communicative potential of teachers' target language use in the foreign language classroom* (Unpublished PhD, Stirling: University of Stirling, 1986)

Mitchell R, *Communicative language teaching in practice* (London: CILT, 1988)

Mitchell R and R Johnstone, 'The routinisation of communicative methodology' in Brumfit C J (ed): 123–43 (1986)

Mitchell R, B Parkinson and R Johnstone, *The foreign language classroom: an observational study.* Stirling Educational Monographs no. 9 (Stirling: Department of Education, University of Stirling, 1981)

Mohan M, 'Classroom management through the target language' in Little D, B Ó Meadhra and D Singleton (eds): 43–47 (1986)

Munby J, *Communicative syllabus design* (Cambridge: Cambridge University Press, 1978)

National Curriculum Council (NCC), *Target practice* (York: NCC, 1993)

Neil P S, *An analysis of teachers' use of the target language with fourth and fifth form German classes* (Unpublished PhD, The Queen 's University of Belfast, 1995)

Neil P S, 'German in the classroom: what the pupils think' in *Language Learning Journal* 13: 10–15 (1996)

Northern Ireland Curriculum Council (NICC), *Guidance materials: modern languages* (Belfast: NICC, 1992)

Nunan D, *Designing tasks for the communicative classroom* (Cambridge: Cambridge University Press, 1989)

Office for Standards in Education (OFSTED), *Modern foreign languages: a review of inspection findings 1993/94* (London: HMSO, 1995)

Parkinson B, D McIntyre and R Mitchell, *An independent evaluation of 'Tour de France'.* Stirling Educational Monographs no 11 (Stirling: Department of Education, University of Stirling, 1982)

Perren G E (ed), *Foreign languages in education.* NCLE Papers and Reports 1 (London: CILT, 1979)

Pride J B and J Holmes, *Sociolinguistics: selected readings* (Harmondsworth: Penguin Education, 1972)

Richards J C (ed), *Understanding second and foreign language learning: issues and approaches* (Rowley, MA: Newbury House, 1978)

Richards J C and T S Rodgers, *Approaches and methods in language teaching* (Cambridge: Cambridge University Press, 1986)

Richards J C and R W Schmidt (eds), *Language and communication* (London and New York: Longman, 1983)

Rutherford W and M Sharwood Smith, *Grammar and second language teaching: a book of readings* (New York: Newbury House, 1988)

Salters J, P Neil and R Jarman, 'Why did French bakers spit in the dough?' in *Language Learning Journal*, 11: 26–9 (1995)

Sanderson D, *Modern language teachers in action* (University of York: Nuffield Foundation, 1982)

School Curriculum and Assessment Authority (SCAA), *Modern foreign languages in the National Curriculum. Draft proposals* (London: SCAA, 1994)

Scottish Office Education Department (SOED), *Report of the Tast Group on modern European languages* (Edinburgh, HMSO, 1991)

Sidwell D and P Capoore, *Deutsch Heute I and II.* Neue Ausgabe. (Walton-on-Thames: Thomas Nelson and Sons Ltd, 1991)

Smith M, *Speakers' Corner.* Association of Teachers and Lecturers Report, November 1993, 13 (1993)

Swan M, 'A critical look at the communicative approach 1' in *English Language Teaching Journal*, 39, 1: 2–12 (1985a)

Swan M, 'A critical look at the communicative approach 2' in *English Language Teaching Journal,* 39, 2: 76–87 (1985b)

Trim J L M, *Some possible lines of development of an overall structure for a European unit-credit scheme for foreign language learning by adults* (Strasbourg: Council of Europe, 1978)

Trundar E, 'Culture crash' in *Times Educational Supplement,* 25 June 1993, Modern Language Supplement, 1 (1993)

Van Ek J A, *The threshold level for modern language learning in schools* (London: Longman, 1976)

Van Lier L, *The classroom and the language learner: ethnography and second-language research* (London and New York: Longman, 1988)

Voss B (ed), *Unterrichtssprache im Fremdsprachenunterricht* (Bochum: AKS-Verlag, 1986)

Westhoff G, *So klug als wie zuvor? Über den Beitrag der Wissenschaft zur Effektivität des DaF-Unterrichts.* Paper delivered at X. Internationale Deutschlehrertagung, Leipzig, 2–7 August 1993 (1994)

Wilkins D A, *Notional syllabuses* (Oxford: Oxford University Press, 1976)

Wing B H, *The languages of the foreign language classroom: a study of teacher use of the native and target languages for linguistic and communicative functions* (Unpublished PhD, Michigan: Ann Arbor University, 1980)

Wong-Fillmore L, 'When does teacher talk work as input?' in Gass S M and C G Madden (eds): 17–50 (1985)

Wragg E C, 'Interaction analysis in the FL classroom' in *Modern Language Journal,* 54, 2: 116–120 (1970)

Yalden J, *The communicative syllabus: evolution, design and implementation* (New York: Pergamon, 1983)

Appendix A

Details of schools and teachers

Teacher 1

Sex	Female
Qualifications	BA (Hons.) Fr/Ger
Main language	German
Number of years teaching	8
Number of years at this school	5
School type	Grammar
Class 1	
Form	5
Number in class	17
Started German in form	3
Number of periods per week	7
Length of period	20 mins
Coursebook	*Deutsch Heute* (rev. ed)
	Schwarz, Weiß, Gold
Chapter reached	DH I and II completed

Teacher 2

Sex	Female
Qualifications	BA (Hons) Fr/Ger
Main language	German
Number of years teaching	3
Number of years at this school	2
School type	Grammar
Class 2	
Form	4
Number in class	24
Started German in form	3
Number of periods per week	8
Length of period	20 mins.
Coursebook	*Deutsch Heute* Ib (rev. ed.)
Chapter reached	15/16

Teacher 3

Sex	Female
Qualifications	BA (Hons.) Fr/Ger
Main language	Equal Fr/Ger
Number of years teaching	16
Number of years at school	12
School type	Grammar

Class 3

Form	4
Number in class	17
Started German in form	2
Number of periods per week	5 per 2 weeks
Length of period	1 hour
Coursebook	*Deutsch Heute* II (rev. ed.)
Chapter reached	3

Teacher 4

Sex	Female
Qualifications	BA (Hons.) Fr/Ger
Main language	German
Number of years teaching	8
Number of years at this school	2
School type	Grammar

Class 4

Form	4
Number in class	28
Started German in form	2
Number of periods per week	8
Length of period	20 mins.
Coursebook	*Deutsch Heute* II (first ed.)
Chapter reached	1

Teacher 5

Sex	Female
Qualifications	BA (Hons) Fr/Ger
Main language	Equal Fr/Ger
Number of years teaching	11 approx.
Number of years at this school	5

School type — Grammar

Class 5

Form	5
Number in class	18
Started German in form	2
Number of periods per week	8
Length of period	20 mins.
Coursebook	*Deutsch Heute* II and III
	Blickpunkt Deutsch

Teacher 6

Sex	Female
Qualifications	BA (Hons) German
Main language	German
Number of years teaching	16
Number of years at this school	5

School Type — Grammar

Class 6

Form	4
Number in class	17
Started German in form	2
Number of periods per week	5
Length of period	35 mins.
Coursebook	*Deutsch Heute* II (first ed.)
Chapter reached	10

Teacher 7

Sex	Male
Qualifications	BA (Hons) Fr/Ger
Main language	German
Number of years teaching	17
Number of years at this school	17
School type	Grammar

Class 7

Form	4
Number in class	26
Started German in form	2
Number of periods per week	4
Length of period	2 @ 35 mins.; 2 @ 40 mins.
Coursebook	*Deutsch Heute* II (rev. ed)
Chapter reached	4

Teacher 8

Sex	Male
Qualification	BA (Hons.) Fr/Ger
Main Language	German
Number of years teaching	8
Number of years at this school	5
School type	Grammar

Class 8

Form	5
Number in class	20
Started German in form	3
Number of periods per week	4
Length of period	40 mins.
Coursebook	*Deutsch Heute* II (rev. ed)
Chapter reached	DH II finished parts of DH III

Teacher 9

Sex	Female
Qualifications	BA
Main language	German
Number of years teaching	16
Number of years at this school	14
School type	Grammar

Class 9

Form	4
Number in class	21
Started German in form	2
Number of periods per week	5
Length of period	35 mins.
Coursebook	*Deutsch Heute* II (rev. ed)
Chapter reached	4

Teacher 10

Sex	Female
Qualifications	BA (Hons.) Fr/Ger
Main language	German
Number of years teaching	19
Number of years at ths school	19
School type	Grammar

Class 10

Form	4
Number in class	12
Started German in form	2
Number of periods per week	4
Length of period	35 mins
Coursebook	*Deutsch Heute* II (rev. ed)
Chapter reached	3

Appendix B

Teacher self-report sheet

German in the classroom
Teacher self-report sheet

Please circle the number which best describes your normal practice for the following content areas with your present 4th/5th form pupils (i.e. the project class)

Key	0	English 100% of the time	
	1	English 75%	German 25%
	2	English 50%	German 50%
	3	English 25%	German 75%
	4	German 100%	

1	Greeting/settling the class	0	1	2	3	4
2	Introducing the lesson objectives	0	1	2	3	4
3	Giving instructions for routine class activities, e.g. pairwork	0	1	2	3	4
4	Moving from one activity to another	0	1	2	3	4
5	Explaining vocabulary	0	1	2	3	4
6	Giving instructions for tests	0	1	2	3	4
7	Explaining grammar	0	1	2	3	4
8	Explaining examination techniques	0	1	2	3	4
9	Praising pupils	0	1	2	3	4
10	Correcting pupil error	0	1	2	3	4
11	Teaching background facts	0	1	2	3	4
12	Disciplining pupils	0	1	2	3	4
13	Summarising points	0	1	2	3	4
14	Asking questions on a text	0	1	2	3	4
15	Giving out homework	0	1	2	3	4
16	Relating activities to pupils' own lives	0	1	2	3	4
	Any other activities (please list)					
17		0	1	2	3	4
18		0	1	2	3	4

Thank you for your help.

Appendix C

Graphs of teachers' self-reports

Teacher 1 self-report

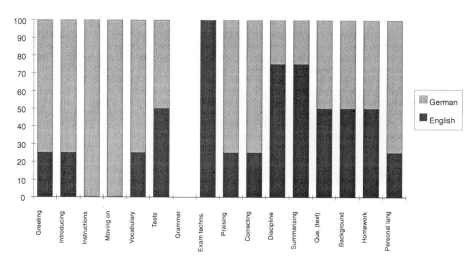

Teacher 2 self-report

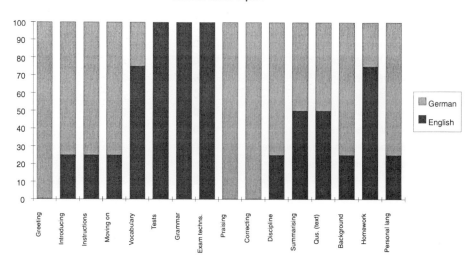

Teacher 3 self-report

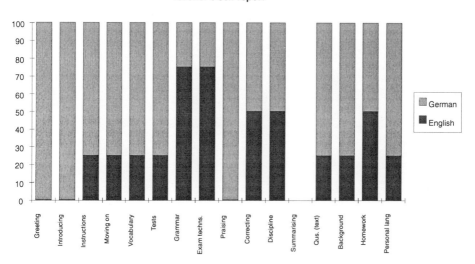

Teacher 4 self-report

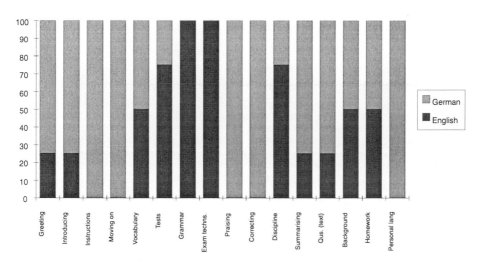

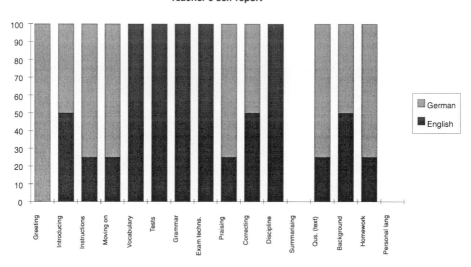

Teacher 5 self-report

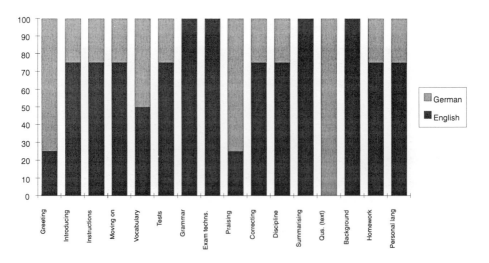

Teacher 6 self-report

Teacher 7 self-report

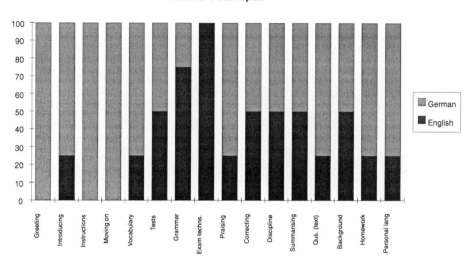

Teacher 8 self-report

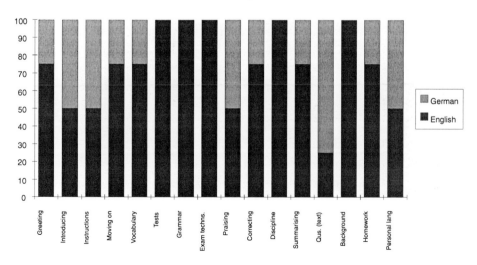

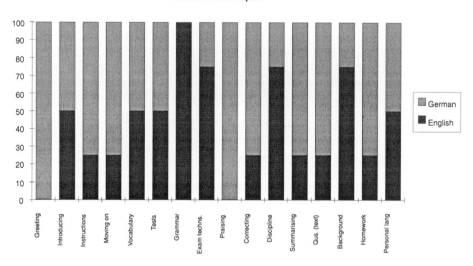

Teacher 9 self-report

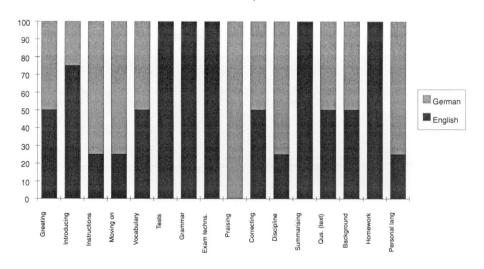

Teacher 10 self-report

Appendix D

Pupil questionnaire

Please take a couple of minutes to answer the following questions. The information will be used for a German project in Queen's University, Belfast. Most answers can be given by ticking the correct box.

1 Your age: _____ Your Form: 4th ☐ 5th ☐

2 Male ☐ Female ☐

3 Your school: Grammar ☐ High school ☐

4 What language or languages are you learning?

German	☐	Irish	☐
Italian	☐	French	☐
Spanish	☐	Other	☐

*In answering the following questions refer to **German** only:*

In which form did you start German? _____

When your teacher does the following things in class, does he or she use English or German?

5 Giving instructions to the class or the group about what they have to do next.

English ☐ German ☐

6 Explaining the grammar — not just giving examples

English ☐ German ☐

7 Telling you what homework you have to do.

English ☐ German ☐

8 Telling you about the foreign country and its people.

English ☐ German ☐

9 Telling you to get out your books, or close your books, or to listen or read or come out to the front of the class etc.

English ☐ German ☐

10   Telling pupils off for being noisy or behaving badly.

English ☐   German ☐

11   How much German does your teacher normally use in class?

English ☐   German ☐

12   How much German would you like your teacher to use in class?

English ☐   German ☐

13   How much of what the teacher says in German do you understand?

English ☐   German ☐

Would you **prefer** your teacher to use English or German when he or she is doing the following things?

14   Giving instructions to the class or the group about what they have to do next.

I would prefer this in: English ☐   German ☐

15   Explaining the grammar — not just giving examples

I would prefer this in: English ☐   German ☐

16   Telling you what homework you have to do.

I would prefer this in: English ☐   German ☐

17   Telling you about the foreign country and its people.

I would prefer this in: English ☐   German ☐

18   Telling you to get out your books, or close your books, or to listen or read or come out to the front of the class etc.

I would prefer this in: English ☐   German ☐

19   Telling pupils off for being noisy or behaving badly.

I would prefer this in: English ☐   German ☐

20   When you are working with a partner, do you speak German:

All the time ☐   Most of the time ☐   Some of the time ☐

Very seldom ☐   Never ☐

21   When you are working in groups in the language class, do you speak German:

All the time ☐   Most of the time ☐   Some of the time ☐
Very seldom ☐   Never ☐

22   When the teacher puts a question in German to other pupils (not to you) do you answer it in your head :

All the time ☐   Most of the time ☐   Some of the time ☐

Very seldom ☐   Never ☐

23   Is there anything else you would like to say about using German either by you as a pupil or your teacher?

Thank you for your co-operation.

Appendix E

Graphs of pupils' views

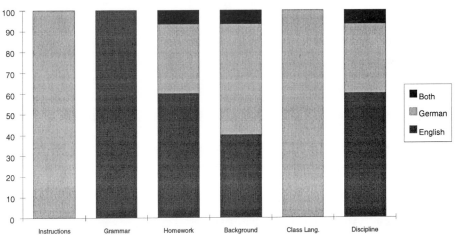

Pupil view Teacher 1

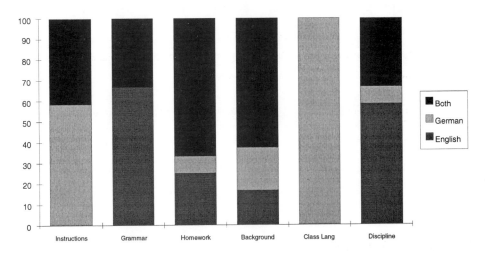

Pupil view Teacher 2

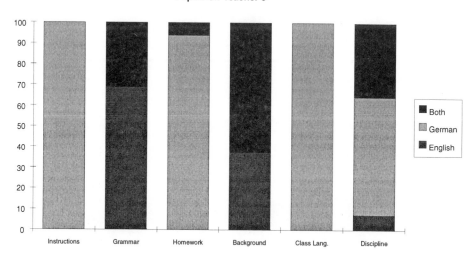

Pupil view Teacher 3

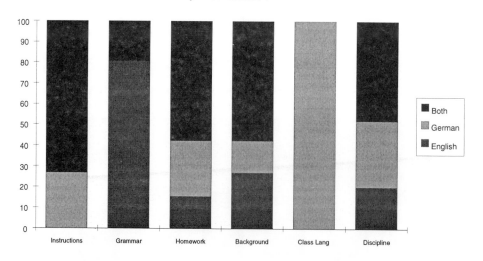

Pupil view Teacher 4

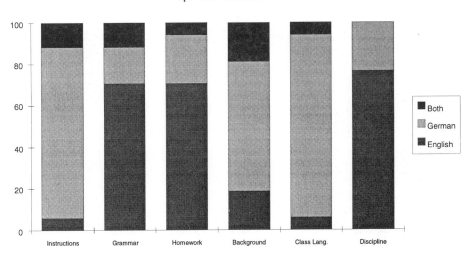

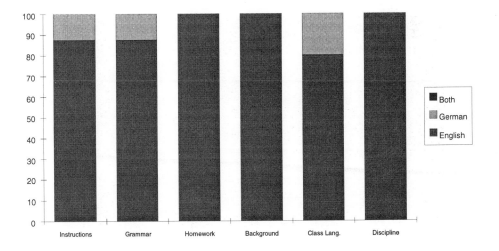

Pupil view Teacher 7

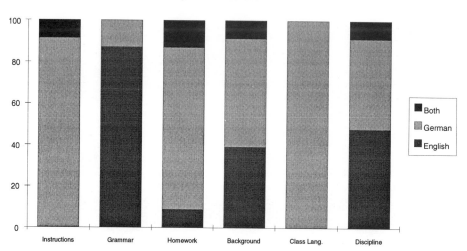

Pupil view Teacher 8

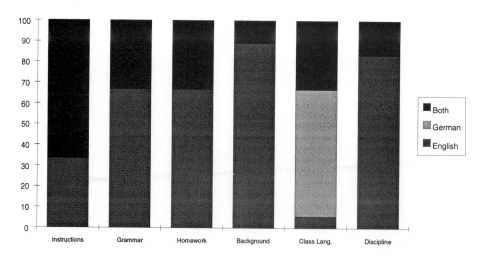

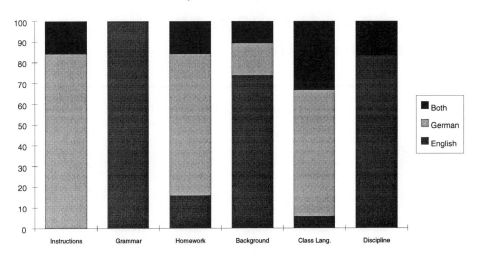

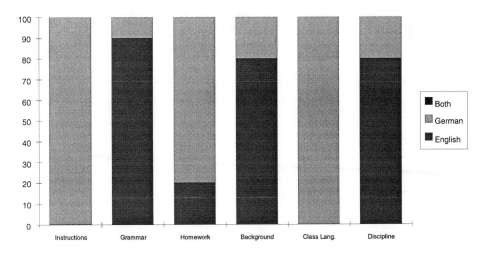

Appendix F

Graphs of teachers on observation data

NB: content areas which did not feature as part of the recorded lessons appear as blanks on the graphs.

Teacher 1 observed

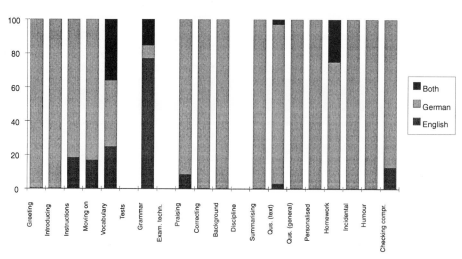

Teacher 2 observed

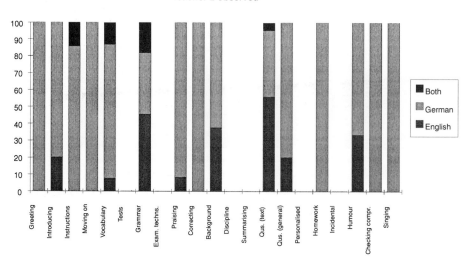

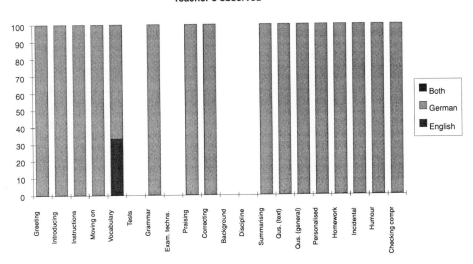

Teacher 3 observed

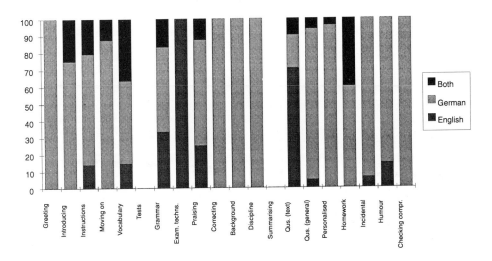

Teacher 4 observed

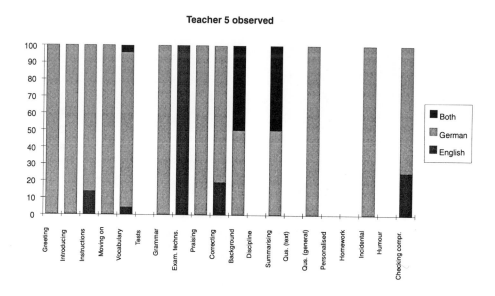

Teacher 5 observed

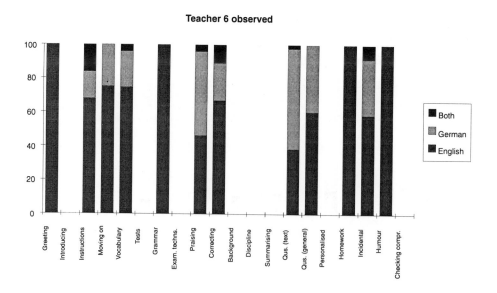

Teacher 6 observed

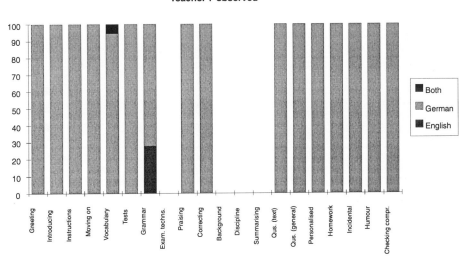

Teacher 7 observed

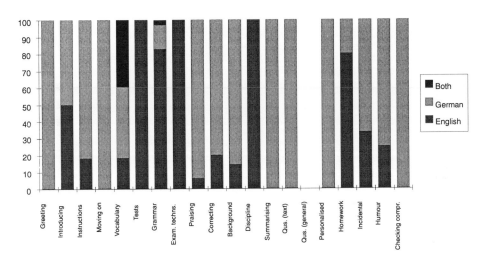

Teacher 8 observed

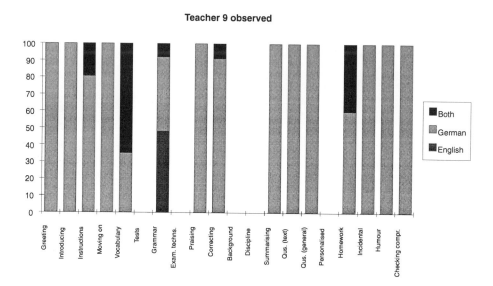

Teacher 9 observed

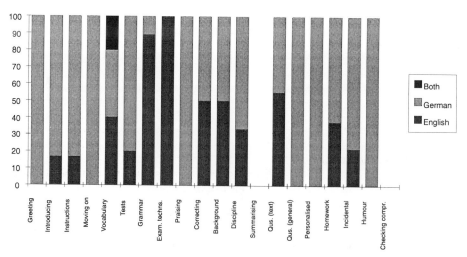

Teacher 10 observed

Appendix G

Previous studies on the target language

Of the various studies which have been carried out into the use of the target language in recent years (Wing, 1980; Hyltenstam, 1983; Mitchell, 1986, 1988; Franklin, 1990; Håkansson, 1986; Guthrie 1987; Duff and Polio, 1990; Hedderich, 1992; Macaro, 1995; Dickson, 1996), only three were conducted within the UK foreign language classroom (Mitchell, 1986, 1988; Franklin, 1990 and Dickson, 1996). Earlier studies, which focused on more general issues relating to the teaching of languages, also commented on the use of the target language as an indicator of good practice (Burstall et al, 1974; Carroll, 1975; Parkinson et al, 1982; Sanderson, 1982). Burstall et al (1974), for example, evaluating the teaching of French in the primary school, commented that in classes where the teacher made much use of the foreign language there was a high correlation with learner use and that both had a positive effect on pupil achievement. Carroll (1975), in an investigation into the teaching of French in eight countries, found a positive correlation between listening proficiency and use of the foreign language in class.

Parkinson et al (1982) in their evaluation of the *Tour de France* project found that the use of French in many schools was restricted to the function of greetings. It must be pointed out, however, that the *Tour de France* was a revolutionary course, one of the first of its kind, appearing as it did in the early 80s, when the use of *Bonjour* and *Au Revoir* in class would have represented a significant increase in the amount of target language compared to earlier methods where virtually no communicative use was made of the foreign language in class either by teacher or by pupil.

In order to put into perspective the findings of the school classroom-based studies, some results from university-based studies are presented; they reveal a wide variation in target language use at that level. Guthrie (1987), for example, found that use of the target language varied between 59-98% in French classes at university. Duff and Polio (1990), investigating thirteen language classes taught by native speakers, found an even greater variation, from 10% at the lower end to 100% target language use at the other. Hedderich (1992), examined the linguistic and communicative use of German by teachers who were using an accelerated language course in Higher Education and found that, in the hypothetical average class, the teachers spoke 59% of the time with half of that time (29.6%) in English and 29.06% of the time in German. It was also found that German was used more in the linguistic mode (16%) than communicatively (13%).

The first major study into the use of the target language in the classroom was conducted by Wing (1980), who concentrated on Spanish teaching in the US. Part of the study involved asking teachers to rate themselves on a self-report sheet on various functions and noting the extent to which they carried out these functions in Spanish or English. The findings revealed a set of classroom activities which appeared to be to be carried out frequently in the target language, such as the limited activities of 'greeting', 'praising' and 'routine instructions', whereas other activities were less frequently conducted in the foreign language such as 'grammar' and 'discipline'. It is worth noting, however, that there was still a relatively high number of teachers using the target language above 50% of the time to perform those functions. Wing found that teachers' use of the target language in practice varied greatly. She divided the fifteen teachers observed into three groups representing high, average and low target language users. Average users spoke in the target language for slightly more than half of the time and slightly less than half of the time while in the communicative mode. High target language users tended to use the foreign language more to explain the linguistic content, than did average or low users. Low target language users tended to spend more of the time talking in the linguistic function and using the mother tongue. Only in talking about personalised topics did the low target language users score above a third of the time (42.5%). The conclusion one might reach from these findings is that practice does not conform to the notion that the target language should be used 100% of the time. In interpreting these data, however, one must take into consideration the fact that the study was done in the US in the late 70s.

The study by Mitchell (1986, 1988) was conducted in Scotland in the early 80s with teachers of first and second year French classes. Mitchell asked teachers if they thought it was feasible to conduct certain functions in the foreign language or in English. This is a slightly different question from that asked by Wing in that it asks teachers about a hypothetical situation rather than about details of current practice. The findings reveal certain similarities to Wing's data, however, in that the 'easy' activities, such as 'informal talk' and 'instructions' were listed by teachers as possible in the target language, whereas the more difficult activities such as 'grammar', 'background', 'objectives' and 'disciplining' were regarded as better done in English. Mitchell comments that although teachers believed that it would be possible to carry out certain functions in the foreign language, this was not always reflected in their practice. Most teachers questioned felt guilty that they were not using the target language as much as they would have liked, although in many cases they felt they were using it as much as they felt to be possible. Only very few stated that the target language could or should be used as the sole means of communication (Mitchell, 1988: 28).

Franklin's (1990) study provides an interesting comparison to Mitchell's, in that it was based in the same context, but at a time when communicative language teaching was no longer a novelty. Franklin also asked which areas of classroom activity could or should be done in the target language. She adds a category, namely, using the target language with difficulty.

The activities which were perceived as most difficult to conduct in the target language were the teaching of grammar and discussing objectives. This mirrors the opinions of teachers in the other two studies presented above. One difference between the two Scottish studies is the much higher percentage of teacher response to using the target language in Franklin's data. She comments that 90% of all teachers recognised the importance of teaching in the target language, although they commented on a hierarchy of difficulty. One possible explanation for the increased percentage in teachers' perceptions of target language use in Franklin's study is that teachers are now much more *au fait* with communicative methodology.

The survey conducted by Dickson (1996) revealed that 89% of teachers regarded it as either difficult or very difficult to teach grammar in the target language, 66% said the same about 'disciplining' and 63% noted the same for 'explaining meanings'. At the other end of the scale 88% stated that it was either very easy or quite easy to 'ask questions' in the target language and 80% stated the same about 'directing pupils'.

TARGET LANGUAGE STRATEGIES

In some of the research (Mitchell, 1985b; Mitchell et al, 1981; Duff and Polio, 1990) various strategies were identified as used by high users of the target language. The main features of modification observed in the Stirling Communicative Interaction Project (Mitchell, 1985b) are worth noting in full:

- repetition
- substitution by using synonyms or associated words
- explanation
- contrast
- exemplification
- clue-giving
- decoding
- interpretation
- pupil interpretation
- teaching explanation in target language with help in MT.

Teachers involved in the Duff and Polio (1990) study at university level, who used the target language 90+% of the time, suggested several strategies which might be used to encourage more target language use:

1   make input comprehensible through verbal modification, such as repetition, reduced speed, paraphrase, simplification of syntax, use of high frequency patterns and routines;
2   use gesture, visuals, mime;
3   video-tape lessons for self evaluation;
4   establish a target language policy from the start;
5   establish a brief period when both teachers and students can clarify material from the lesson, which helps reduce anxiety;
6   emphasise the fact that all language does not need to be understood;
7   explicitly teach and use grammatical terms in the target language from the beginning;
8   provide supplementary grammatical material in English.

(adapted from Duff and Polio, 1990)

CONCLUSION

One might conclude from the details in this section that teachers are now much more confident about using the target language for certain aspects of the lessons, but that they still feel there are certain activities which are best done in English. The results of the present study support this view.

Biographical notes

Professor Richard Johnstone is Head of the Department of Education, University of Stirling, and Director of Scottish CILT. He has directed many research projects for SOIED on the teaching and learning of foreign or second languages, and has written several books on the subject. His most recent work has included responsibility for the evaluation of national pilot projects in modern languages in Scottish primary schools.

Dr Peter Neil is currently Director of Northern Ireland CILT and Director of the Centre for Modern Language Teaching at the Queen's University of Belfast where he has responsibility for the pre- and in-service training of modern language teachers. Born on the Scottish island of Bute he studied at the universities of Edinburgh and Glasgow, trained as a teacher at Jordanhill College, Glasgow and taught languages in five Scottish comprehensive schools. He has also been involved in GCSE and 'A' level German examining with two examination boards. His main research interests are input in foreign language classrooms and diversification.